The
POWER
of
PERSUASION

The
POWER
of
PERSUASION

*Improving
Your Performance
and Leadership
Skills*

Rupert Eales-White

**KOGAN
PAGE**

ACKNOWLEDGEMENTS

Thanks to Chantal James for her hard work and dedication, to Peter Herriot, Carole Pemberton and Roger Harrison for their constructive comments and to Thomas Frame, John Van Maurik, Grahame Murphy and David Butler for their contribution.

Kogan Page Limited
120 Pentonville Road
London N1 9JN

© Rupert Eales-White, 1992

British Library Cataloguing in Publication Data

A CIP record for this book is available from the British Library.

ISBN 0 7494 0957 6
    0 7494 0682 8 pbk

Typeset by Saxon Printing Ltd, Derby

Printed and bound in Great Britain by Biddles Ltd., Guildford and Kings Lynn.

CONTENTS

◆ Introduction ◆

From the cradle to the grave, we try to influence how others think, feel and behave. Equally others do the same to us.

When a baby is hungry, it cries. This is quite persuasive as the parents are disrupted, find the crying irritable and have an incentive to feed the baby so that the crying ceases.

Wherever there is interpersonal contact, whether in the business, social or partnership context, persuasion is all pervasive.

The frustrations and stress that come our way as a result of a perceived lack of success or success that is defeated by time and the individual concerned have a marked impact on the quality of our lives and on the achievement of goals and ambitions we hold dear.

The power of persuasion is unarguable. However, what is also true is that the individual often has little control over the outcomes and little understanding of why his particular approach has not always been successful.

For example, many individuals discover that a particular approach can be successful in a certain situation or with a certain individual, and yet the same approach is unsuccessful in a different situation with the same person or in a similar situation with a different individual.

Also, what can happen is that the approach seems to be successful and the 'persuadee' gives an oral commitment: ie 'Yes, I will do what you want me to do and I agree with the course of action'. However, much to the chagrin and annoyance of the 'persuader', who believes that her persuasion approach has been successful, the oral commitment remains just that. There is no follow-up action consistent with the promise made.

These outcomes are not surprising and are not a matter for criticism. The skills of managing interpersonal relationships effectively (of which persuasion is one of the most important) are not explicitly taught to us in our formative years. They are not part of any core or non-core school curriculum and few parents sit their children down and say, 'Over the next few months we will teach you all aspects of persuasion and develop your knowledge and skills base so that the effectiveness with which you manage relationships is significantly enhanced!'

We learn, or are even indoctrinated, in an implicit and un-structured way rather than being educated in an explicit and structured way, with the necessary skills development part of that explicit education process.

This book is an attempt to eradicate the gap that exists for most – to help the individual develop knowledge and skills and hence become more successful in harnessing the power of persuasion.

A subsidiary theme of the book is leadership, because how we persuade has an impact on how we lead. Increasing recognition is being given to the manager's role as leader and follower rather than technical or professional expert or administrator. The book should provide valuable help in improving our competence in these 'people' roles.

This is not an academic book but a practical book with a practical approach. So we start with the ILEG Inventory, where you look at a set of statements and decide whether you agree or disagree. Your answers determine your persuasion profile.

Next we develop knowledge by examining the nature of each persuasion approach, the meaning and origin, the language we use when operating in a particular approach, and the strengths and drawbacks.

We then look at different mixes that produce different profiles, the impact of the size and shape of the profile and how the same score in an individual style can provide a different emphasis, depending on which questions were answered in the affirmative.

We move on to consider the nature of leadership, and the different types of leader the persuasion profile can indicate. We examine the historic leadership role-model, its relevance today, and what research shows current leadership approaches are, and what the future might hold.

So the first part of the book enables you to uncover where you are coming from and why, by providing a framework for personal analysis, and then considering how that framework can help you determine your current perspective, the historic reasons for that perspective and your current competence.

The next part of the book concentrates on skills development. We look first at the one-to-one situation, and examine the critical skills of effective listening and questioning. Then we look at the group situation and you as leaders, persuading the group. The key skills examined in detail are creativity and facilitation.

Next we consider the persuasion meeting – the many formal

occasions when we are trying to persuade a colleague, client, superior or subordinate to do what will help us achieve our goals. We look at objective-setting and two useful models that will assist in that process. We look at how to plan, prepare, structure and manage the meeting in a way that will optimise our chances of success.

In the penultimate chapter on practice, we examine a real-life role play dealing with a business problem, taking the actual language used, examining how and why the outcomes were less than desired and pointing out the language and approach that would produce a successful outcome.

Finally, we look at how we can improve in those areas where we have decided we want to improve.

The focus of the book is on the business environment – how we can develop and deploy skill on the back of self-perception to enable us to be more effective in our interactions with our colleagues, subordinates and clients generally and more competent and confident in our leadership role specifically.

However, inevitably, any benefits that are derived and skills effectively deployed in the business environment will have an equal impact on social or partnership relationships.

1

◆ How Do You Persuade? ◆

The first step in discovering how effective and skilful you are in persuading others is to produce a profile of the mix of persuasion styles that you deploy. Different individuals have different mixes and different emphases, have different understandings and perceptions and different levels of competence and skill.

Until we understand how we persuade, why we persuade the way we do, and how effective our current approaches are, we cannot improve our knowledge and develop our skill. In short, until we know where we are, we cannot decide where we want to be, and how to get there.

So I ask you to fill in what I call the ILEG Inventory. The use of the mnemonic ILEG will become clear, as soon as the profile has been produced. The word 'inventory' is partly training jargon (which I will keep to a minimum) and partly reflects the reality that it is not a questionnaire, but a list of statements, where you have the choice to agree or disagree.

There are sixty such statements and before you start I provide five guidelines.

- Be totally honest. Otherwise the exercise is pointless. There are no right nor wrong answers, just a learning experience – and no one is looking over your shoulder!
- Do not think too much. Go with the flow of your initial instinctive feeling.
- Think of how you are when at work. In the vast majority of responses, there will be an identity between work and elsewhere. However, this is a work-based inventory. So some of the statements will not easily translate to the social or relationship areas.
- Some questions assume that you have responsibility for staff. For these, choose the current situation if you have and if you have not, imagine that you have, and answer as honestly as you can.
- Some questions assume that you work in a group, if not

regularly then at least occasionally. If you are a group or team leader, answer in that capacity. Otherwise answer as a team or group member.

So make your decisions. If you agree with the statement more than disagree, tick the agree box. If you disagree more than you agree, tick the disagree box.

For all statements, a choice is required.

Have fun!

THE ILEG INVENTORY

	Statement	Agree	Disagree
1.	I have been told I help others grow and develop in their jobs	☐	☐
2.	I give emotionally more than I receive	☐	☐
3.	I regularly check others do what they have said they will do	☐	☐
4.	I am more logical than creative	☐	☐
5.	I enjoy the cut, thrust and heat of a good argument	☐	☐
6.	I keep my staff under control	☐	☐
7.	I value and respect people, who have different views and attitudes to my own	☐	☐
8.	I listen to and comfort a member of staff who is upset	☐	☐
9.	I prefer to work in a team rather than on my own	☐	☐

Statement	Agree	Disagree
10. I deal better with people's feelings than with facts	☐	☐
11. Using facts and logic is the way I persuade other people	☐	☐
12. I motivate staff, using goals and targets	☐	☐
13. I discipline a member of my staff who makes mistakes	☐	☐
14. People let me down, facts don't	☐	☐
15. I listen to and support people who disagree with me	☐	☐
16. I put forward ideas to which the group becomes committed	☐	☐
17. I use my authority to ensure my staff meet their targets	☐	☐
18. Getting the facts right is vital to persuading another person	☐	☐
19. I persuade individuals in the group to share information	☐	☐
20. I welcome criticism and feedback on my performance	☐	☐
21. I prefer action to planning	☐	☐
22. I expect people to perform to my standards	☐	☐

	Statement	Agree	Disagree
23.	We cannot rely on the present or the past, if we are going to be successful in the future		
24.	I have been told that I am a good listener		
25.	I put forward strong logical arguments		
26.	Consensus is more effective than competition		
27.	I ensure my staff know what's expected of them and how their performance will be measured		
28.	When with another person, I listen more than talk		
29.	I am quick to criticise others, when they make mistakes		
30.	If I don't understand and respond to the other person's point of view, I can't persuade him to mine		
31.	If I'm sure of my facts, it's almost impossible to budge me		
32.	I prefer ideas to facts or opinions		
33.	I easily handle any challenge to my views		
34.	Most decision are taken by my team and not myself		

Statement	Agree	Disagree
35. Work is only effective if there is a solid structure and discipline	☐	☐
36. I put others' interests above my own	☐	☐
37. If I get the facts right and build up a strong logical case, I win the argument	☐	☐
38. I am quick to praise another for her good perfomance	☐	☐
39. I prefer to work with the team rather than the individual	☐	☐
40. I put more effort into developing another's ideas than my own	☐	☐
41. I think there is some merit in the saying 'spare the rod, spoil the child'	☐	☐
42. I am quick to admit mistakes to others	☐	☐
43. I prefer to talk about my views rather than listen to others talking about theirs	☐	☐
44. I persuade others through creating a shared vision and understanding	☐	☐
45. I use my authority to provide necessary discipline	☐	☐
46. I prefer to be part of group creativity sessions to thinking on my own	☐	☐

Statement	Agree	Disagree
47. If you haven't done thorough research, you won't be able to persuade me	☐	☐
48. I ask others to express their thoughts, feelings and opinions to me	☐	☐
49. I am interested in and promote another's ideas and suggestions	☐	☐
50. Analysis and logic is the way to solve problems	☐	☐
51. I discipline poor performers	☐	☐
52. I focus on the goals of the group to persuade an individual member	☐	☐
53. I expect to be praised for a job well done	☐	☐
54. People tell me I help others more than myself	☐	☐
55. I paint an exciting picture of what could be rather than what is	☐	☐
56. I push my views strongly	☐	☐
57. Competition is more effective than co-operation	☐	☐
58. I like to be in charge	☐	☐

Statement	Agree	Disagree
59. When I win, you win and vice versa	☐	☐
60. Teamworking is the way forward	☐	☐

SCORING THE INVENTORY

There are 60 questions, with numbers from 1 to 60. These have been split below into four equal sets of 15 numbers. There is an I set, an L set, an E set and a G set.

There are nine steps. An example is provided for an individual, called EP, to whom we will return later on. The numbers and sets for you to use are on pages 18 and 19.

- Go through your answers, starting at the beginning.
- Ignore all the Disagree boxes.
- Identify the number corresponding to each tick in an 'agree' box.
- Underline the corresponding number, which will be found in one of the four sets.
- Continue until you have finished.
- For each of the four rows of numbers, add up the number of underlinings and put the total in the corresponding box.
- Add up the total of the four boxes, as a checking mechanism.
- Go back to the inventory, and add up the number of ticks. If that total equals the total of the ILEG boxes, you have finished.
- If it does not, you will have to check back to find and rectify the error.

EP example

<u>3</u> <u>6</u> <u>12</u> <u>13</u> <u>17</u> <u>22</u> <u>27</u> <u>29</u> <u>35</u> 38 <u>41</u> <u>45</u> <u>51</u> <u>53</u> <u>58</u> | 14 | I

4 <u>5</u> 11 <u>14</u> <u>18</u> <u>21</u> <u>25</u> <u>31</u> 33 37 <u>43</u> <u>47</u> <u>50</u> <u>56</u> <u>57</u> | 13 | L

2 8 10 15 20 <u>24</u> 28 30 36 40 42 48 49 <u>54</u> 59 | 2 | E

<u>1</u> 7 9 <u>16</u> <u>19</u> <u>23</u> 26 32 34 39 44 46 52 <u>55</u> 60 | 5 | G

Total = 34

Your scores

3 6 12 13 17 22 27 29 35 38 41 45 51 53 58 | | I

4 5 11 14 18 21 25 31 33 37 43 47 50 56 57 | | L

2 8 10 15 20 24 28 30 36 40 42 48 49 54 59 | | E

1 7 9 16 19 23 26 32 34 39 44 46 52 55 60 | | G

Total =

PRODUCING YOUR PROFILE

EP's profile has been produced as an example (Figure 1). Figure 2 is for you to produce your own profile.

The steps are:

1. Take your I score, and put a small cross where it comes on the I part of the IE, or horizontal, axis of the profile. The 15 numbers available are marked out from the centre to the end of each leg – I on the horizontal left, L on the vertical top, E on the horizontal right, and G on the vertical bottom. EP's score was 14.

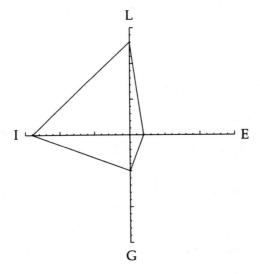

Figure 1 EP's profile

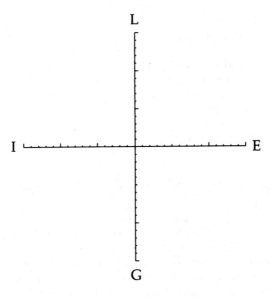

Figure 2 Your own profile

2. Repeat the exercise for the other three scores – the L score, the E score and the G score. EP's scores were 13, 2 and 5.

3. Take a ruler, and join up the crosses to produce the profile.

INTERPRETATION

Now, the next two chapters provide a structured and detailed analysis of how to interpret the profile, a necessary precursor to the subsequent chapters on knowledge and skill development. However, I think it would make a lot of sense, and put the whole profile into a meaningful context, if we started at the end.

In other words, I will examine three different profiles, actual profiles of real people, as if I was in a counselling or advisory role, and we were having a detailed discussion of the profiles as part of a growth and development experience, to which each individual was committed.

I will deal in objective terms, as if all I saw was the profile, and did not know the person. Before I start, there are two fundamental points, which individuals who want to be trained and 'certified' to use my inventory must bear in mind.

■ The scores and, particularly, the mix provide clues, but only clues. The counsellor must not make assumptions, but question the manager or other individual to uncover and agree the realities to which the clues lead. Only with a clear mind, an objective and empathetic approach can that base of understanding and acceptance be achieved.

■ In real life situations, it may be necessary to refer back to the answers to identify which aspect of the particular approach is more dominant or suppressed.

Mary

Mary's scores were I = 5, L = 7, E = 13 and G = 4. Her profile is set out in Figure 3.

The first thing to notice is the very high E score. E stands for *Empathy*. The ability to be able to listen to and understand other people is a very powerful force indeed, both in having effective relationships and being able to persuade. It is a 'you and I' style of persuasion. It can be an assertive style ie a style of persuasion and behaviour based on respecting your rights as wells as the other person's. It provides the capability to enter another's world, and

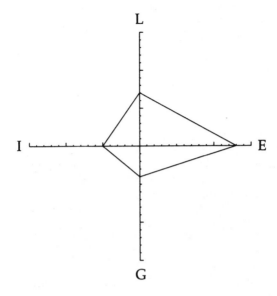

Figure 3 Mary's profile

pull him or her towards yours, through the trust and understanding generated.

However, while it is never an aggressive style, it can be a submissive or non-assertive style. Instead of 'you and I', it is 'only you'. This possibility is indicated by a high score. While it is indicated, the possibility only becomes a probability, depending on how *Dominant* that style is. Now, the gap between Mary's E score, and the next highest score, the L score of 7, is 6, large enough to indicate an E dominance, and a tendency towards non-assertive behaviour, as well as assertive behaviour.

Now, I should not turn round to Mary, and tell her that 'her problem is that she is too submissive'. That would be an ego-style approach. The two ego styles are L = *Logic*, and I = *Incentives*. While an element of E improves the power of all other styles, people, where dominant in one style, tend to appreciate someone 'coming from the same style' – and Mary's style is Empathy!

So I would need to explore, with a high level of listening skills and open questions, such matters as:

■ how easy does she find it to delegate? If she finds it hard, why does she think that that is the case?;
■ how easy does she find it to say no to her boss?;

- does she find that she does her colleagues' work, and perhaps even her subordinates' work occasionally? (Any closed questions leading to a yes or no answer would be followed up by open questions to explore the reasons, the circumstances and how happy she is with the outcome.);
- how many hours does she put in at work?;
- does she do much teamworking? What is her approach?; And so on.

This would lead to a recognition of development areas, and the reasons. While one, assertiveness, sticks out, there might well be others such as time management, focusing on prioritisation, systems and delegation.

If Mary is a team leader, the profile provides insights and perspectives on leadership as well. Figure 4 shows Mary's profile in leadership form, with four quadrants – control, support, vision and motivation. The detail is set out in Chapter 4. Put simply, a combination of Incentives and Logic indicates a control orientation, a combination of Logic and Empathy a support orientation, a combination of Group focus and creativity with Empathy a vision orientation, and a combination of Group with Incentives a motivation orientation.

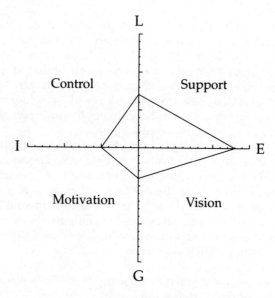

Figure 4 Mary's leadership profile

Key features of this profile, which would be tested out in the course of the feedback and development discussion, are as follows.

There is a high support quadrant, but the other quadrants are less significant, particularly the motivation quadrant. It looks as if Mary finds it difficult to provide a structure of incentives, targets and goals, and cannot exercise control easily. She does not appear to be comfortable with team interactions generally nor trying to generate a shared vision of the purpose and direction of the team.

She appears much more comfortable with supportive one-to-one interactions. She may well lack confidence in her role, partly because of where she is coming from, and partly from lack of effective training, support and guidance from her company.

In addition to assertiveness, a course covering basic team leadership skills and techniques (such as group brainstorming) should provide the catalyst to greater confidence and competence in her role.

A final point, before we move on to John. While a high E score may indicate lack of assertiveness, even so there will often be success ie a voluntary movement towards the position of the persuader ie Mary (provided her requirements have been determined and articulated by her) due to the affection and trust in which she is held by the persuadee (ie the person being persuaded).

John

John's scores were I = 7, L = 9, E = 6, and G = 14.

His persuasion profile is set out in Figure 5.

The initial striking feature here is the very high G score. The group style denotes the use of concepts and ideas to *pull* the individual towards a shared vision of the future, not just predicated on the attitudes or perceptions of the two individuals interacting. It is deployed by someone who believes in and promotes teamworking and the pursuit of the common aspirations and goals the team can develop and share. A very high G score also indicates a well-developed creative ability.

However, in John's case, it is a dominant style, with a gap of 5 before the *secondary style* in Logic (9). The E score is a moderate 6. The push total (the combined I and L scores) is 16, compared to the pull scores (the combined E and G scores) of 20. The gap between the two is small, and the push score dominated by G.

Therefore, there is a possibility, to be explored with John, that he can lapse into aggression on occasions, and has a tendency to confuse the 'vision' and his ego. Instead of being 'let us work together towards our group goals of effective service to our

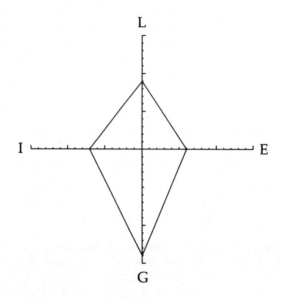

Figure 5 John's profile

customers', it becomes 'let us work together to achieve my vision for the team or my future'.

Equally, looking at the leadership profile (Figure 6), there is a strong vision quadrant and motivation quadrant. However, the motivation could be based on the ego as much as the vision ie setting the targets and goals for the team, rather than agreeing them with the team on the basis of shared understanding and commitment.

Two worries I would have with John as a leader are:

■   He might be charging down the hill, whilst the rest of his team were still climbing to the top.
■   He would be in danger of demotivating an immature team, through expecting too much of them, and not spending the time and effort (E = 6) to coach them effectively.

EP

You may recall EP's scores; I = 14, L = 13, E = 2, and G = 5. The persuasion profile is set out again in Figure 7.

I have used the initials EP as this is a generic profile that a number of managers and other individuals have. EP stands for ego persuader. There is a double dominance in the two ego or push

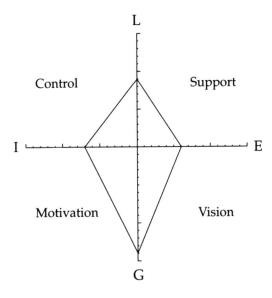

Figure 6 John's leadership profile

styles – logic and incentives. Both styles can be very effective. Using logic and data is an approach that is inbuilt into our educational system of persuasion. 'Sticks and carrots', targets and objectives are inbuilt into our parental and organisational system of persuasion.

There are also major limitations on effectiveness.

The combined dominances indicate an individual who is locked into his view of the world. They indicate an individual of strong views, opinions and prejudices. Where the mind is made up, it becomes a closed world. The persuasion approach is to force another by the power of logic, the power of facts and data, the power of the stick and the carrot, the power of position and authority to accept, agree and conform.

It is a combination that most of us deploy some of the time, and some of us deploy most of the time.

It is the explanation of why, when the persuader uses that combination of persuasion styles, the persuadee will sometimes agree orally – the lowest level of behavioural commitment – and fail to follow up!

The leadership profile is set out Figure 8.

As is to be expected, the control quadrant reigns supreme. If EP

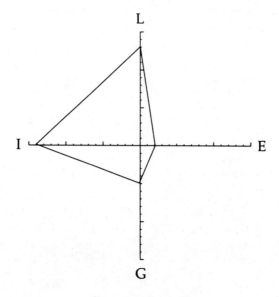

Figure 7 EP's profile

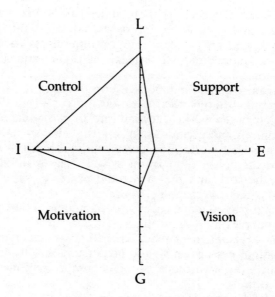

Figure 8 EP's leadership profile

was the managing director of a company, I would expect the following characteristics:

- Not a team player!
- Not a strategic thinker.
- In addition to a short-term focus, likely to concern himself with capital and financial issues, rather than IT issues (probable area of ignorance and hence uncertainty, which is not psychologically permitted) and human resource (HR) issues!

These three profiles have provided a glimpse of the end and, I hope, an incentive to continue with the beginning!

The next two chapters cover in more detail and structure each style and various style mixes.

Before turning to these chapters, I have a suggestion to make. It would be very valuable for you if you got a colleague at work who knows you well and who is important to you (perhaps your boss) to fill in the inventory – not for himself or herself but to provide his or her perception of your approach to persuasion.

The reason is simple. There can be gaps between how we see ourselves and how others see us.

There can be great value in identifying any gaps that do exist, exploring the reasons why and implementing strategies to close them.

The 'other' version is set out on the following pages.

THE ILEG INVENTORY (OTHER)

Statement	Agree	Disagree
HE OR SHE:		
1. Helps others grow and develop in their jobs		
2. Gives emotionally more than he receives		
3. Regularly checks others do what they have said they will do		

Statement	Agree	Disagree
HE OR SHE:		
4. Is more logical than creative	☐	☐
5. Enjoys the cut, thrust and heat of a good argument	☐	☐
6. Keeps her staff under control	☐	☐
7. Values and respects people who have different views and attitudes to his own	☐	☐
8. Listens to and comforts a member of staff who is upset	☐	☐
9. Prefers to work in a team rather than on his own	☐	☐
10. Deals better with people's feelings than with facts	☐	☐
11. Persuades other people using facts and logic	☐	☐
12. Motivates staff, using goals and targets	☐	☐
13. Disciplines a member of his staff who makes mistakes	☐	☐
14. Thinks that people let her down, facts don't	☐	☐
15. Listens to and supports people who disagree with him	☐	☐

Statement	Agree	Disagree
HE OR SHE:		
16. Puts forward ideas to which the group becomes committed	☐	☐
17. Uses her authority to ensure her staff meets their targets	☐	☐
18. Thinks that getting the facts right is vital to persuading another person	☐	☐
19. Persuades individuals in the group to share information	☐	☐
20. Welcomes criticism of and feedback on his performance	☐	☐
21. Prefers action to planning	☐	☐
22. Expects people to perform to her standards	☐	☐
23. Believes that we cannot rely on the present or the past, if we are going to be successful in the future	☐	☐
24. Is a good listener	☐	☐
25. Puts forward strong logical arguments	☐	☐
26. Believes that consensus is more effective than competition	☐	☐
27. Ensures his staff know what's expected of them and how their performance will be measured	☐	☐

Statement	Agree	Disagree

HE OR SHE:

28. Listens more than talks when with another person

29. Is quick to criticise others, when they make mistakes

30. Believes that if she doesn't understand, and respond to other' points of view, she can't persuade them to her own

31. Is almost impossible to budge if sure of his facts

32. Prefers ideas to facts or opinions

33. Easily handles any challenge to her views

34. In the main, lets his team take decisions

35. Believes that work is only effective if there is a solid structure and discipline

36. Puts others' interests above his own

37. Wins the argument if she gets the facts right and builds up a strong logical case

38. Is quick to praise others' for their good perfomance

Statement	Agree	Disagree
HE OR SHE:		
39. Prefers working with the team than the individual	☐	☐
40. Puts more effort into developing anothers' ideas than his own	☐	☐
41. Thinks there is some merit in the saying 'spare the rod, spoil the child'	☐	☐
42. Is quick to admit her mistakes to others	☐	☐
43. Prefers to talk about his views rather than listen to others talking about theirs	☐	☐
44. Persuades others through creating a shared vision and understanding	☐	☐
45. Uses her authority to provide necessary discipline	☐	☐
46. Prefers to be part of group creativity session than thinking on his own	☐	☐
47. Will not be persuaded by someone who has not carried out thorough research	☐	☐
48. Asks others to express their thoughts, feelings and opinions to her	☐	☐

Statement	Agree	Disagree
HE OR SHE:		
49. Is interested in and promotes another's ideas and suggestions		
50. Believes that analysis and logic is the way to solve problems		
51. Disciplines poor performers		
52. Focuses on the goals of the group to persuade an individual member		
53. Expects to be praised for a job well done		
54. Helps others more than herself		
55. Paints an exciting picture of what could be rather than what is		
56. Pushes his views strongly		
57. Believes that competition is more effective than co-operation		
58. Likes to be in charge		

Statement	Agree	Disagree
HE OR SHE:		
59. Believes that when she wins, the other person wins and vice versa		
60. Thinks that teamworking is the way forward		

Your (other) scores

3 6 12 13 17 22 27 29 35 38 41 45 51 53 58   ☐   I

4 5 11 14 18 21 25 31 33 37 43 47 50 56 57   ☐   L

2 8 10 15 20 24 28 30 36 40 42 48 49 54 59   ☐   E

1 7 9 16 19 23 26 32 34 39 44 46 52 55 60   ☐   G

Total =   ____

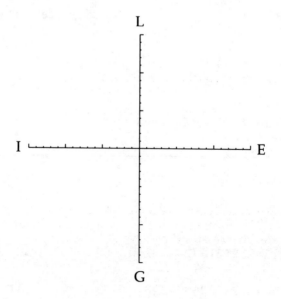

Figure 9 Your (other) profile

◆ The Four Persuasion Approaches ◆

In this chapter, we look at each of the four approaches to persuasion. We consider the meaning and origin, the language we use, the strengths and the drawbacks.

LOGIC

If $X + Y = 5$

and $X - Y = 1$,

Then $X = 3$ and $Y = 2$

Definition

Logic: 'Science of reasoning, proof, thinking or inference ... Correct or incorrect use of reasoning ... Ability in reasoning.'

Reason: 'Intellectual faculty characterised especially of human beings by which conclusions are drawn ... (fact adduced or serving as) motive, cause or justification.'

Concise Oxford English Dictionary

When operating in this mode, an individual makes connections between facts or opinions in a structured way to reach conclusions that it is hoped, nay often expected, will successfully persuade another to his or her point of view.

The expectation is there, because when we use logic to persuade another, we logically think that logic will prevail!

Origin and power

Logic is at the heart of language, and hence communication.

Our education system focuses on logic, not on creativity nor feeling. Logic is the key to acquiring knowledge. From an early age, we learn the importance of facts, the importance of memory to retain facts, how to develop an information base, how to apply logic to facts to reach conclusions that provide new facts that expand our information base, and hence our knowledge.

Logical thinking is a continuous, iterative and sequential process that we undertake most of the time both at the conscious and subconscious levels. Even when we are in an emotional state, we try to verbalise logically. 'Do this because I say so' is giving a reason, even though emotion is driving word and action.

Logic is only suspended when we think creatively – as logic and judgement are the enemies of ideas.

Many of us are taught to worship at the altar of logic. We define an individual as intelligent, not if they have common sense or intuitive skills, not if they have creative or visionary skills, but only if they have logical or rational skills.

Language

'You cannot do that because it is illogical.'
'Logic dictates.'
'You must do this because it will increase productivity.'
'The facts speak for themselves.'
'The results of the cost benefit analysis are clear. You must go ahead with the project.'
'If you close the canteen, you will have a strike on your hands.'
'You can't pour a quart into a pint pot.'
'As we are operating at full capacity, you cannot do your production run.'
'To say that you die before you die is nonsense.'

I have used the last phrase to exemplify how logic is the enemy of creativity. Edward de Bono points out that one way of becoming more creative is to provoke the brain out of the rut of logical thinking, suspend judgement and generate movement to a good idea. The idea will only be recognised as 'good' if it connects back logically. However, it is incapable of being generated by logic in advance.

This particular provocative thought was actually used by an executive working in life insurance in the 1970s. The norm at that time was that the proceeds of an insurance policy were paid out only after the death of the person insured. The key feature was that the person was dead. The executive deliberately reversed that feature (totally illogical of course) to jerk the brain away from logic and assumption.

The result was the launch of a very successful new insurance product, which paid out three-quarters of the death benefit to the terminally ill before they died!

Finally, in this aside, I would point out that humour is a very powerful creative tool (as well as generating an atmosphere in which individuals will be prepared to accept criticism). Think about it. If we knew the punchline in advance, we would not laugh – but we only laugh if we can make logical connections afterwards.

Humour is a creative act.

Strengths

We are all susceptible to the power of logic, as we all think logically.

If someone says to us:

'Here is the situation; here are the facts; this the conclusion that can be drawn from the facts; therefore this is what you should do'; then, *provided*

We are also operating in a logical mode; we agree to the facts; we understand the logic that leads to the conclusion; we will accept the conclusion – *we will be persuaded.*

Drawbacks

A point that holds for all persuasion styles is that if we rely on one style too much, then we will be less successful more often than if we learn to use a mix of styles, choosing the style that matches the situation and the individual or individuals concerned.

We all have feelings and we all dream dreams. If we are in an emotional or creative state, and someone uses logic on us, we will not be persuaded. We might do what they say, however, if they use positional power and incentives in addition. This style is covered in the next section.

A cultural norm (particularly holding for men, who dominate our companies, organisations and institutions and so preserve the norm) is to be more comfortable with facts, analysis and logic, and less comfortable with feelings and ideas.

How often do we say: 'What do you think?' not 'How do you feel?', 'I have an opinion' not 'Have you an idea?'

So logic on its own will persuade only infrequently, the frequency increased when we are persuading someone who tends to have logic as their preferred or dominant style, as they will rarely be in an emotional or creative state.

However if an individual can respond to those operating in other states, he can move them into the logical mode, and into a rational decision-making process, thereby achieving his goals.

There is one final point. If we turn back to the dictionary definition of logic, we notice: 'correct or *incorrect* use of reasoning'.

Logic can be used not to expand knowledge, but to push opinion or promote prejudice. There is a danger that logic is deployed purely from and to support the individual ego. In fact we can become quite illogical when we use logic in this way.

For most of us at times, and for some of us for most of the time, we can be locked into our particular view of the world. We become incapable of any discovery, growth and change process. We use logic to support our view and to try to thrust it on others. Often we fail or our victory is Pyrrhic, unless we have power over them, when we can deploy a mix of incentives to get our own way.

I have met a number of people who have been prone to this type of thinking. It occurs when we are driven by passion, belief or prejudice, masquerading at the conscious level as fact – by a conviction that we know best, we are always in the right, and it is our duty to convert others to our way of thinking.

Examples in public and private life are manifold. One will suffice. Throughout her parliamentary career until 1991, Margaret Thatcher was opposed to referenda. She argued passionately and powerfully that we were a parliamentary democracy, which had both the right and a duty to protect the national interest and its own sovereignty. She decried the suggestion that the Mother of Parliaments should be by-passed in favour of views (taken at but one moment in time) of the population as a whole. Rule by referenda would undermine both good government and parliamentary democracy. Referenda were anathema.

Recently Margaret Thatcher has argued powerfully and passionately that the issue of parliamentary sovereignty and the threat to it posed by European integration is so vital that the only way it can be satisfactorily addressed is by a referendum. On this issue, the people are given no choice as the mainstream parties are all in favour of a measure of integration. In any case, as parties present a menu of policies in their election manifestos, the voter cannot vote effectively on single issues.

This is a classic case of the illogical use of logic or 'incorrect use of reasoning'. The reasons are twofold: she lost the power to control events; depending on our perceptions, more important than Margaret Thatcher's, she has a passionate commitment to her concept of British sovereignty and/or she believes that European integration will destroy our national sovereignty and/or she is prejudiced against Europeans.

INCENTIVES

Definition

'Incitement (to action) ... provocation, motive ... payment or concession to stimulate greater output of workers'.

Concise Oxford English Dictionary

This persuasion approach concerns itself with both means and ends – with incitement to action. An individual operating in this mode will use incentives to persuade another to perform to meet an objective.

Incentives are but one aspect of motivation, though for some, using this mode, they are perceived as the only way to motivate. They can be used in three ways.

■ To persuade another to behave and act in a way that meets the personal goal of the individual deploying them.
■ To persuade another to meet the performance standards, and hence, over time, the objectives that have been set for the individual by his manager – the persuader.
■ As the key element to self-motivation by the 'persuadee' to achieving objectives and performance standards that have been agreed with and are 'owned' by the persuadee rather than set for him.

The incentives deployed can be negative or positive – sticks or carrots. They operate at the emotional level rather than the rational level though, as already mentioned, the language deployed is often logical.

Positive incentives range from monetary to non-monetary (eg status symbols, promotion) to praise or flattery. Promotion usually, but not always, has a monetary aspect as well.

Negative incentives involve threats (open or veiled) or criticism.

Origin and power

As mentioned in the first chapter, incentives are the key tool deployed by most parents and hence organisations to persuade us, when children, to behave and act in the way they want or consider appropriate. From earliest memory we are set goals and performance standards, and the stick and the carrot is deployed to persuade us to perform and achieve. There is, naturally, a continuity of approach when we go to school.

Some favour the stick (literally – although physical punishment tends not to be the cultural norm when we are adults – a sudden, inconsistent and, hence, incomplete switch) and some the carrot.

I met an adult, who was successfully persuaded to eat up all his food, when a child. He believed the threat that, if he did not, he would be beaten up in the middle of the night by a 'big black man'. He also mentioned that he frequently woke up in the middle of the night bathed in sweat and trembling with fear as the result of nightmares, bringing to life the threat.

I have met a child who was successfully persuaded to eat up all his food by his parents. The inducement was that, if he did, he would grow up to be big and strong like his football hero – John Barnes.

Both children were white. The former is racially prejudiced (inevitably) and the latter much less likely to become so, as his father deliberately supported non-white sporting heroes, an example duly followed by the son.

I am sure that each and every one of us has a host of stories to tell about the nature and success of incentives deployed when we were children.

Incentives are very powerful and very effective. They appeal to our emotions. Most of us like praise and many succumb to flattery. The extra money, that key promotion, those ego-satisfying non-financial status differentials (company car, plush office, personal secretary and so on) work their wonders.

So too does that biting criticism, which makes us curl up inside and that frisson of fear that we will lose face, our privileges, even our job.

Language

'Well done. That was an excellent piece of work.'
'Just remember that your annual appraisal is next week.'
'I think your target should increase by 20 per cent, don't you. After all, we have just shed 20 per cent of the workforce.'
'The chairman wouldn't like that suggestion.'
'Could be seen as career regressive.'
'You're the only man for this important project. Your handling of the last one was superb.'
'You must take the job – you'll get that Merc you've always wanted.'
'OK, targets up by 20 per cent, but so too is the bonus if you meet them.'

'Your time-keeping is terrible.'

Strengths

The use of incentives, the need to perform and to achieve targets is a norm for most of us – so we are susceptible to such a persuasion approach, and are often persuaded.

The effectiveness of the approach is enhanced by the existence of positional power, which is often the case. In other words incentives are a frequent mode of persuasion used by our 'bosses' on us, and by us on our 'subordinates' – just as they were deployed by the figures of authority in our childhood – our parents and teachers; just as we, as parents, use them on our children.

Appeals to our basic emotions, aspirations, needs and values are bound to have a significant impact.

Drawbacks

Culturally, if we make any comment on others, we tend to criticise more than praise – subordinates to their face, bosses behind their backs. It is a rule, with but few exceptions, that managers persuading subordinates naturally deploy direct or veiled criticisms and threats when operating in this persuasion mode.

It is almost a behavioural norm that two people – peers – chatting or 'gossiping' together will have but words of praise for each other, and words of criticism for any other names brought into the frame. This also holds for small groups or teams. The production team does not spend much time praising the efforts of marketing, finance, computing or sales! This is a comment, not a criticism.

There are two reasons: it helps build up the personal relationship or team spirit; many of us have fragile egos, are not as confident as we would like to be, however good our external image, and are psychologically bolstered by this process. We are lifted by the mutual backslapping that takes place and by the gap created in our favour between recognition of our worth being made explicit and the recognition of others' flaws being exposed.

However, when we are criticised, we don't like it, we don't like the person criticising us, and we may become bloody-minded and either not be persuaded or do the opposite!

More generally, this style of persuasion tends to be an ego style. When we deploy it, we are often persuading the other person to the targets or performance standards that we or our bosses have set or mandated for them. They are not committed to them in the first place, which makes persuasion unlikely to be successful.

Equally, we can fall into the trap of subconsciously assuming that what makes us tick, the incentives that motivate us, apply to the person we are trying to persuade, which is not always the case!

However, if we have or can develop an empathetic approach, then we are more likely to deploy the right approach to incentives.

EMPATHY

Definition

'The power of entering into another's personality and imaginatively experiencing his experiences ... the power of entering into the feeling and spirit of something and so appreciating it fully'.

Chambers Concise Dictionary

'Power of projecting one's personality into (and so fully comprehending) object of contemplation'.

Concise Oxford English Dictionary

Someone using an empathetic mode of persuasion has moved her centre of attention away from herself and focused her faculties, intellectual and emotional, on the person with whom she is talking. She has become sensitive to the thoughts and feelings of the other person.

By developing and deploying this power, the persuader can pull the persuadee towards his own point of view. Necessarily, there must be a flexibility and openness in the persuader's own thinking and attitudes, so that the final outcome represents the best of both worlds. Both worlds will have changed from their original form as the result of the empathetic persuasion process.

I have quoted two dictionaries in this instance, as Chambers emphasises the need to enter another's world and move away from the ego, whereas the Oxford concentrates on the pull aspects towards the ego base, retained under its definition. I would imagine that the latter was written by an individual or individuals, preferring the ego approaches to persuasion!

Origin and power

Man (and woman) is a social animal. We start off in life with the need to be loved and the need to belong. For those, whose upbringing has not stunted nor distorted these natural human needs, one of the key drivers and goals of life, whether consciously or subconsciously stated, is to form close bonds, warm friendships, with at least one of a sexual nature.

There is great power and personal growth derived from an effective bond with a fellow human being – sharing and caring with another.

Language

'I trust your judgement.'

'How do you feel about this.'

'I understand your position. Let me explain mine.'

'I agree.'

'Oh dear! that must have been a terrible disappointment for you.'

'I would value your opinion on this.'

'I appreciate that status is important to you. Can you appreciate how important it is for me that I improve teamworking.'

'To be honest, I don't feel at all happy about your suggestion.'

'I'd like to hear your ideas first.'

'There is no way that you can cope with that work schedule. Allow me to help.'

Strengths

The fundamental strength of this persuasion style is that it explicitly recognises how important the persuadee is. While we may succumb to logic, work for promotion, or react to threats, we warm to recognition of our value and importance.

We are much more likely to be persuaded, if we have had the opportunity to express our feelings and our views, if we know that they have been respected and appreciated, if we recognise and understand why the other person thinks and feels the way she does, and, finally, if we jointly own a shared decision and course of action.

I mentioned earlier that empathy was powerful and enabled personal growth. It is the nature of empathy that the outcome for the persuader will be different from her original objective.

If the persuader comes to the persuasion interview or discussion with her mind made up, knows the answers and it is just a question of gaining agreement (verbal being sufficient) there will be no empathy, and there will be no learning.

If the persuader comes to the interview with an objective and with a view of what she wants and why, but with the desire and skill to develop empathy, then, if successful, the outcome will be different from the start. The difference may be marginal or significant, depending on the degree of coincidence between the feelings, attitudes and views of both parties, when elicited and how they change as the parties move into empathy.

In an empathetic process, both parties change from their starting points. Those dominated by the ego styles use the word compromise to describe the outcome – but that would be the only word they could use, as that is all they can achieve. Unfortunately our business world is full of compromises that satisfy neither party.

Those that experience the process call it a win/win outcome – where the sharing of feelings, opinions and ideas generates a solution path that is higher or better than either anticipated at the outset.

Two points before we look at drawbacks:

■ A survey into the financial services industry, carried out by Touche Ross in 1987, examined what factors had made for success, as measured by a significantly above average return on equity. When it came to human resources, the factor was empathy. Empathy is good for the bottom line, though in desperately short supply among a large sector of the industry – the banks!

■ The preferred cultural styles of persuasion are logic and incentives, because of the way we are brought up and educated. Women, research has shown, tend to be more empathetic than men. There is therefore a very strong business case for companies to deploy more woman in management and executive positions to increase the empathy levels, the win/win solutions, and hence the bottom line.

Drawbacks

There is no drawback, generally, to being empathetic. Indeed it is a persuasion style that tends to be underdeveloped and underemployed by decision-takers, and one that individually and collectively most of us need to employ more frequently. Additionally, using an empathetic approach at an early stage in a persuasion situation will make our subsequent use of a logical, incentive or group mode of persuasion more effective.

Any generalisation permits exceptions, and this is no exception! There will be occasions when circumstances dictate a lack of empathy. An empathetic process is more time-consuming than the ego approaches. When there is a crisis and the clock stands at one minute to midnight, there will need to be command and control to avert that crisis.

The real drawbacks are when the process is incomplete or excessive. An effective empathetic process is a two-way process – a form of assertive behaviour, where there is a respect by the persuader not only of the views, opinions and feelings of the persuadee, but also of his own.

If the persuader does not bring his own position into play, the persuadee can gain two perceptions of the persuader:

■ A manipulator – someone who is playing their cards very close to their chest. He is opening them up, not reciprocating, and using the resulting information to further his own political aims.

■ A pushover – someone who is basically non-assertive or submissive. Over time, this leads to such people being taking for granted, taken advantage of, and losing self-respect and the respect of others.

As mentioned in the first chapter, a very high, or dominant, E score indicates the latter, and as regards the former, we would need to examine what questions were answered in the affirmative, as well as the scores in the other styles, to gain a little insight. The last section of the next chapter examines this aspect.

GROUP

Definition

This is the persuasion approach of concepts, ideas, dreams and visions. When operating in this mode, we try to pull the persuadee to a common understanding of a shared vision that is fundamentally extrinsic ie lying outside the dictates of the individual egos. To be effective the persuader has to tap into an intrinsic need of the persuadee. This need may be latent ie operating at the subconscious level.

In short, the persuadee is trying to create or harness a group need, vision, direction and focus. She may use this approach to persuade an individual or the group itself.

Origin and power

What differentiates us from the ape? Why have so many given their lives for God or Country? Why did so many believe in and obey Adolf Hitler? Why did so many white people cry when Martin Luther King was assassinated?

We all dream dreams. Many wonder why they are, what little

they know. Many are drawn to concepts, ideas, ideologies and faiths that provide answers. We seek answers that lie beyond ourselves, yet strike a chord within.

The power of the vision defines the power of the group.

Language

'You should agree. It will help the customer.'
'Don't forget. It is a team effort.'
'Let us be client-first.'
'If we do this, we'll stuff the competition.'
'You should share that information. Otherwise our team won't complete the project on time.'
'United we stand, divided we fall.'
'Remember our company's mission.'
'If you do that, you'll let the side down.'
'What about a team motto: quality through equality.'

Strengths

The greatest strength is in group interactions, rather than one-to-one interactions. However, because of our intrinsic need to belong, and the desire that most have for fulfilment beyond mere self-interest, it can be a very effective persuasion approach at the individual level. This is especially true if there is also an initial use of empathy.

Drawbacks

There is a darker side to this group approach. While the focus of this book is on work groups from the team to the department to the company itself, we all know the damage caused at national level when the vision appeals to and excites our baser rather than our nobler instincts.

If we look back to John's profile in Chapter 1, we will recognise that the vision and the ego can coincide. As was the case with empathy, there can be a manipulation of others' emotions to achieve personal goals.

It is a moot point whether, when using a style incorrectly or in excess, it is better to ignore others' emotions using logic or incentives, or unleash and corrupt them using empathy or group.

CONCLUSION

We have looked at each style – what it means, where it comes from, and the strengths and drawbacks. This was a necessary first step, but assumed that we operate in one style only. This is rarely the case. We deploy a mix of styles, which makes us more effective in our persuasion than relying just on one.

More importantly, whatever mix we currently deploy, we all have the capability to accentuate the positive aspects of each approach, to develop strengths where there are now gaps and to develop technique and skill so that we achieve a significant increase in effectiveness.

The next step on the road is to look at the persuasion profile and what it means. This forms the content of the next chapter.

3

◆ The Persuasion Profile ◆

To start our examination of the profile, ie the mix of the four persuasion approaches, we look at strength classification. We then move on to look at the focus of the profile, the impact of the size and shape of the profile, and how the same score in an individual style can provide a different emphasis, depending on which questions were answered in the affirmative.

Strength classification

Range of scores	Classification
12–15	Dominant
8–11	Strong Preferred or Secondary
4–7	Moderate
0–3	Weak

Let us develop our understanding by examining the menu of possibilities.

SINGLE DOMINANCE WITH NO SECONDARY

I set out an example in Figure 10, which I have called the cold fish. The scores taken are I = 5, L = 12, E = 3, G = 3.

We see that this individual's persuasion approach is dominated by logic, and there is no strong support nor secondary in any other

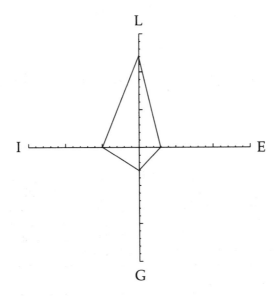

Figure 10 The cold fish dominance

style. Such an individual is likely to be a very introverted and dry character. He could be quite competitive, but only at the intellectual level.

There is no desire to control others, an inability to relate to others on a one-to-one basis, little creativity and no drive towards some externally focused dream or vision. He would not be a team player. Such individuals could be found in many walks of life eg scientist, accountant, lawyer.

The three other single dominances are set out in Figures 11, 12 and 13 – the bulldozer (dominant I), the pushover (dominant E) and the visionary (dominant G). Dealing briefly with each:

The *bulldozer* rolls over people with the power of authority, the drive for control and the emphasis on discipline, with an overt use of the stick and the carrot. Not a subtle person – focuses on the individual he wants to dominate, using the force of personality and power to get his own way, without resource to logically consistent argument. ' Do this or else '; ' but why?'; 'because I say so'.

The *pushover* (like Mary) focuses on individual relationships, but this time in order to please and be loved. She gives way, and plays a supporting subdominant role, not infrequently in an unhealthy alliance with the Bulldozer, where there is compatibility.

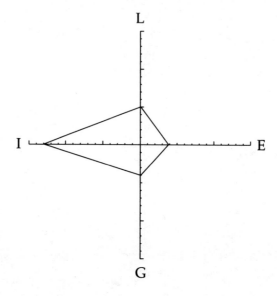

Figure 11 The bulldozer dominance

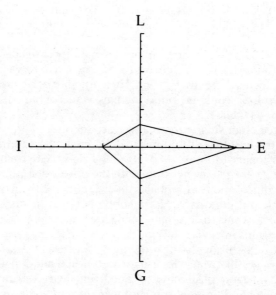

Figure 12 The pushover dominance

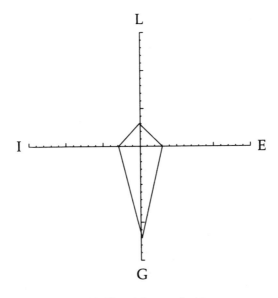

Figure 13 The visionary dominance

The *visionary* is a highly creative, imaginative and inspirational individual – fundamentally group orientated rather than interested in the individual. He focuses on creating a shared vision of something new, without regard to reality and the individual need. In companies, he would be a rebel with a cause, but without connections.

DOUBLE DOMINANCE WITH NO SECONDARY

We have examined an example of this – the ego persuader. There is only one other double dominance possible and that is Empathy and Group – someone who has been called to care *and* has creative visionary strengths. Most such individuals would in fact have a dominance in E and a secondary in G (or even a moderate score), rather than a dominance. The reason is provided in the penultimate section of this chapter 'Deeper Aspects'. Such individuals would be found in the caring professions or vocations – teachers, nurses, doctors, clergymen etc.

The reason that there cannot be any other double dominance is

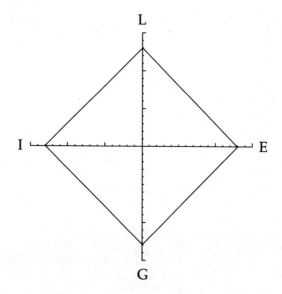

Figure 14 The self-deceiver profile

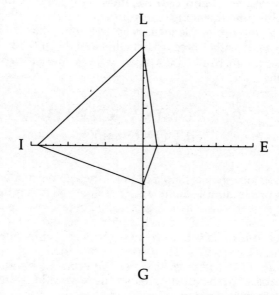

Figure 15 The ego persuader

that an individual cannot be both strongly internally focused and strongly externally focused. That does not mean to say that I have not seen triple dominances, and quadruple is possible. The generic title I have given to such profiles is self-deceivers, shown in Figure 14.

Let us have some fun with a possible candidate – Robert Maxwell. From all the reports I have read, he was undoubtedly dominant in Incentives – using the stick and the carrot unsparingly. He was also likely to have been dominant in Logic, with a dollop of the rational, and a large tranche of the unreasonable or prejudicial. In short, a competitive control merchant par excellence. Not a team player, as evidenced by his approach to pension fund decisions(!), although could well have a moderate score in G, with some visioning skills. A low E score, I fancy. These are set out in Figure 15.

So can we accept Maxwell as an ego persuader?

However, if our Robert had filled in the inventory, he might well have come out as a quadruple dominance. It is a reality that those with dominants in the ego styles or dominant in one, with a secondary in another, who are in positions of power and control, tend to deceive themselves.

This is because of the ivory tower syndrome, coupled with a well-developed tongue from subordinates. I have seen it time and time again. 'You're a real team player, boss!' 'So many good ideas.' 'What breadth of imagination, what vision.' 'Typical of you to be so sensitive and caring.' And so on, ad nauseam!

Ego persuaders tend to believe the lines they are fed, and there is no-one to tell them the truth or, if someone does, exit left! The temporary wound that could lead to a perception closer to reality is soon bathed and soon heals.

If a reader has such a profile, and has not torn up this book, may I recommend that you ask a peer or superior (not a subordinate!) who knows you well to fill up the appropriate 'other' questionnaire. You can then compare his or her perceptions of you as a persuader with your own. There will be a gap, and it might be worth recognising this reality, and moving forward.

You are only old once.

DOMINANCE WITH A SECONDARY

Taking the case of a single dominance, then if the next score is in the moderate or weak range, the implication is that the individual relies very heavily on that style or approach. It is the natural or

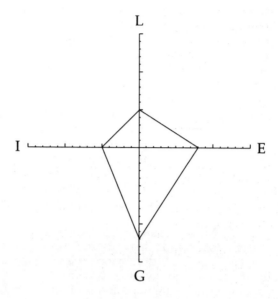

Figure 16 The inspirer

automatic style adopted. As said before, each style can be very powerful, and an individual dominated by one approach can be effective.

However, as also indicated, what will be perceived as an effective approach by the individual concerned will often be perceived completely differently by other people, particularly those with different profiles. Someone dominant in Logic will be perceived as unfeeling and unemotional by someone dominant in Empathy, will be perceived as uncaring, unimaginative, and excessively individualistic by someone dominant in Group, and as stubborn and unreasonable by someone dominant in Incentives.

One of the themes covered in Chapter 9 (The Persuasion Meeting) is the need for many to develop flexibility in approach. The capability is improved where the dominant style has a supporting style or secondary (scores in the range 8 to 11). What this means is that effectiveness is improved as the number of people and situations where the combination is appropriate increases.

We have already seen an example of such a combination in John in Chapter 1, who was dominant in Group with a secondary in Logic. Another example would be the Inspirer, dominant in

Group, with a secondary in Empathy. The profile, with moderate scores in Logic and Incentives, is set out in Figure 16.

This would be the profile of Martin Luther King or Jesus Christ, with the positive, ennobling vision for mankind as a whole (the dominant style) supported by the ability to care and relate to the needs of the individual.

PREFERRED STYLES

Many people do not have a dominant style, whether supported or not. As we have seen, being dominant in a style can have a major impact on effectiveness. The profiles of many have one or more preferred styles (scores 8 to 11) with secondaries in the moderate range or other scores in the weak range. There is a diminution in intensity and power of the individual approach but a greater balance and a greater capability of flexibility. Also, when we look to the individual questions, there may be a particular focus within a given approach.

I provide one example in Figure 17 – the assertive persuader, with preferences in Logic and Empathy, and moderate scores in Incentives and Group.

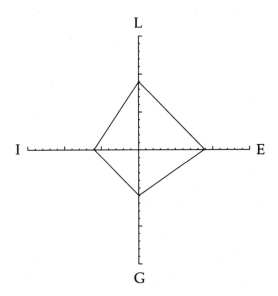

Figure 17 The assertive persuader

Such individuals are not significantly into power and control, nor are they particularly creative or visionary. Their emphasis is on one-to-one relationships, where they are often effective persuaders. They deploy the two key characteristics of assertive behaviour – respecting and asserting their own rights and viewpoints and, at the same time, respecting the rights and viewpoints of the individual with whom they are interacting. On an individual basis, they have the capability of generating win/win outcomes – (see Chapter 9).

FOCUS

You may recall that I used the words push to describe the Incentives and Logic approach to persuasion and pull to describe the Empathy and Group approaches. What I mean is that, when deploying Logic or Incentives, we tend to push the individual towards our position, without necessarily understanding his or her position. When using Empathy or Group, we tend to pull the persuadee towards a common understanding or shared vision through entering her world or creating a new world based in part on her existing world.

If we take the difference between the two scores on an individual profile, we can gain some understanding of the direction and intensity of the individual focus. If we start with the pull scores (E + G), and subtract the pull scores (I + L), a positive difference indicates an external focus, and negative difference an internal focus.

The measures of intensity are set out below.

Focus range	Intensity
1 to 5	Weak
6 to 10	Moderate
11 to 15	Strong
More than 15	Excessive

What does this all mean?

Remember the ego persuader's scores in Chapter 1; I = 14, L = 13, E = 2 and G = 5.

The pull scores (E + G) = 7. The push scores (I + L) = 27. The

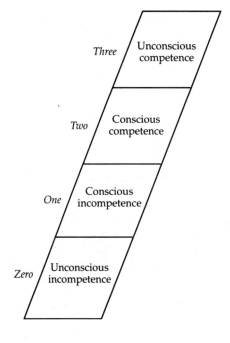

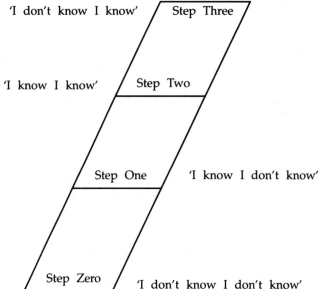

Figure 18 The learning ladder

difference is –20 or (20). This individual, and others with the same or similar profiles, is excessively internally focused. They are driven by their needs and perceptions, by the desire to gain power and exercise control and are often very successful, with the price seemingly paid by others. Robert Maxwell is an example of the reality of the ultimate situation which is lose/lose.

The inspirer's focus was external, with a score of 14. This is a strong external focus ie the subordination of personal needs to the needs of the group and the individual, with the emphasis on the needs of the group.

The assertive persuader's focus is (with the scores taken) zero – a state of balance.

Incidentally, questionnaires and inventories that ask us how we think, feel and behave are useful, but their value should not be overstated. What they do is reflect back to us what we already know, but sometimes have forgotten. More importantly, they put that knowledge into a structure and context that is new to us. That is their power, as they enable us to gain a greater self-knowledge than we had before, a greater understanding of not only what we are but why we are what we are. That is the necessary precursor to improvement.

They enable us to consciously recognise what our strengths and weaknesses are in the areas addressed, whereas before that recognition may have been latent or subconscious. We change from not knowing we did or did not know to now knowing. The next step in this learning ladder is to gain conscious competence in the areas of incompetence through the application of skill in the real world. At this level, we know that we know. Finally we reach the highest level, automatic or subconscious competence – we do not know that we know! This process is set out on the charts in Figure 18.

Questionnaires and inventories can be shafts of light in a darkened room, but can never be the sun. I make this point strongly now, as there is a danger that I am trying to be too scientific and too prescriptive. This is not the intention. The degree of focus merely provides a clue, of which you will know the relevance and usefulness.

SIZE AND SHAPE

The shape of the profile is much more important than the size. If our E score is much higher than our I score, that has significance.

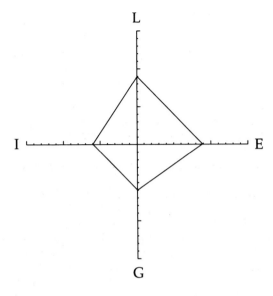

Figure 19 The assertive persuader

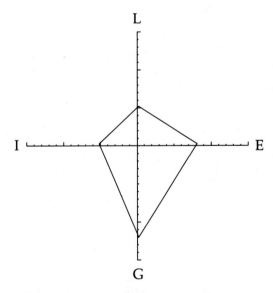

Figure 20 The VTL

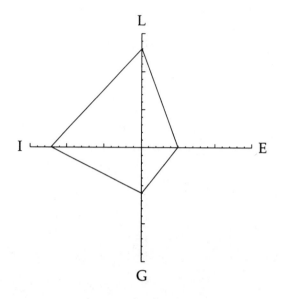

Figure 21 Confident

If our profile covers the entire area, that means we have deceived ourselves!

However, there can be indications of confidence and competence through combinations of the size and shape of the profile. Confidence and competence are indicated by a fairly balanced shape of moderate to large size, such as the assertive persuader or a profile strong in the G quadrant such as the Visionary Team Leader, covered in the next chapter on leadership (see Figures 19 and 20).

Confidence alone is indicated by a high internal focus ie with the profile skewed towards I and L. Lack of confidence is indicated by a strong or dominant E score and moderate to low scores in the other quadrants ie a skewed and small shape. These two examples are set out in Figures 21 and 22.

DEEPER ASPECTS

In this section, we recognise that raw scores, their combination and the variation in size and shape of the profile, provide valuable but limited insights. An individual can score, say, 9 under Empathy

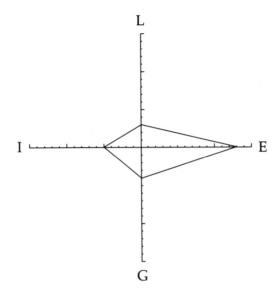

Figure 22 Lacking confidence

and yet have a significantly different emphasis in this persuasion style from an individual with exactly the same score.

So we examine the subclassifications under each umbrella heading to see how these variations occur and what they mean.

Incentives

The stick and the carrot is deployed to achieve and maintain control, to encourage performance, to motivate, and to discipline. Each aspect is examined with the emphasis on control and discipline, because of cultural norms. Praise and criticism are also covered. There is an element of overlap in the subclassifications, and selection is based on where the greatest emphasis is given.

Control:

3. I regularly check others do what they say they will do.
6. I keep my staff under control.
17. I use my authority to ensure my staff meet their targets.
58. I like to be in charge.

Discipline:

13. I discipline a member of my staff who makes mistakes.

35. Work is only effective if there is a solid structure and discipline.
41. I think there is some merit in the saying 'spare the rod, spoil the child'.
45. I use my authority to provide necessary discipline.
51. I discipline poor performers.

Performance:

22. I expect people to perform to my standards.
27. I ensure my staff know what's expected of them and how their performance will be measured.

Praise:

38. I am quick to praise another for his good performance.
53. I expect to be praised for a job well done.

Criticism:

29. I am quick to criticise others when they have made mistakes.

Motivation:

12. I motivate staff, using goals and targets.

So what, I hear you ask. In fact, this question and why? are perhaps the most important questions we should ask of ourselves, others and anyone who is trying to persuade us!

Why do you think that?
So what does that mean?
So what assumption are you making?
I see. So why do you make that assumption?

These are examples of open questions covered in Chapter 6.

Let us take two individuals with a preference in Incentives and a score of 9.

One score excludes all the discipline statements and the criticism statement. The other excludes all the control statements, the motivation and the praising others statement.

The first person likes to be in control, to be in the know, uses the carrot rather than the stick – is not keen on discipline to achieve that control. Control is helped by the setting of targets, goals and performance standards. However, if control is to be successful in the absence of discipline, then I would expect this individual to have moderate or strong scores in some of the other quadrants. As this is an ego style, it is likely that there would be a strong Logic score as well. They often, but not always, go together. Those with a high Incentives score tend to have a high Logic score. Less so in the reverse – witness the assertive persuader and John. Remember the cultural, and hence corporate and individual, bias towards Incentives and Logic.

The second person is a disciplinarian, but not a control merchant. He has probably had a very disciplined upbringing, with the regular use of the 'stick', and that is his own persuasion approach at work.

He does not consciously push for control or power, purely for a disciplined, certain environment.

These are two hypothetical individuals with incomplete scores. However, the analysis shows how the same score produces significantly different emphases. If the score is in the weak or dominant range, then the differences are much less significant.

Logic

The five subclassifications are pure logic, facts, facts and logic, comparative and competitive.

Pure Logic:

25. I put forward strong logical arguments.
50. Analysis and logic is the way to solve problems.

Facts:

18. Getting the facts right is vital to persuading another person.
31. If I am sure of my facts, it is almost impossible to budge me.
47. If you haven't done thorough research, you won't be able to persuade me.

Facts and Logic:

11. Using facts and logic is the way I persuade other people.
37. If I get the facts right, and build up a strong logical case, I win the argument.

Comparative:

4. I am more logical than creative.
14. People let me down, facts don't.
21. I prefer action to planning.

Competitive:

5. I enjoy the cut, thrust and heat of a good argument.
33. I easily handle any challenge to my views.
43. I prefer to talk about my views rather than listen to others talking about theirs.
56. I push my views strongly.

57. Competition is more effective than co-operation.

Let us again take two individuals, with a preference in logic, and a score of 9. The first excludes the competitive statements and the action statement. The second excludes the facts, and facts and logic statements, and the comparative factual statement.

The first is likely to be a highly developed rational logical thinker, perhaps a cold fish, with moderate or weak scores in the other categories. The second is likely to be a more prejudicial thinker, arguing from belief, prejudice or opinion – without much recourse to the facts of the matter. The second individual could well have a preference in Incentives, as he is developed in the emotional side of logic rather than the rational side.

Empathy

I use five classifications – Assertive, Listening, Comparative, Subdominant and Neutral.

Assertive:

20. I welcome criticism of and feedback on my performance.
30. If I don't understand and respond to the other person's point of view, I can't persuade her to mine.
42. I am quick to admit my mistakes to others.
48. I ask others to express their thoughts, feelings and opinions to me.
59. When I win, you win and vice versa.

Listening:

 8. I listen to and comfort a member of staff, who is upset.
15. I listen to and support people who disagree with me.
24. I have been told that I am a good listener.

Comparative:

10. I deal better with people's feelings than with facts.

Subdominant:

 2. I give emotionally more than I receive.
28. When with another person, I listen more than talk.
36. I put others' interests above my own.
40. I put more effort into developing another's ideas than my own.
54. People tell me that I help others more than myself.

Neutral:

49. I am interested in and promote another's ideas and suggestions.

Again, let us take two individuals with identical E scores of 9. The first excludes all the subdominant statements and the comparative statement. This individual is likely to have a balanced empathetic approach – the ability to enter another's world, while retaining a focus on his or her own interests, opinions and perspectives, a necessary precursor to achieving dipolar synergy ie a win/win outcome that is of greater quality than the initial stances of the two individuals interacting.

The second individual excludes all the assertive statements, and the neutral statement. He or she is likely to fall into the pushover category.

A final point. You may recall that in Chapter 2, I stated that a dominant E score suggests a non-assertive approach. This is inevitable, as a score of 12 would include at least one subdominant statement, and is likely to include more, if not all.

I also mentioned the manipulator, who is likely to have a moderate score in E, focused on asking others for their points of view and being a good listener.

Group

The four classifications used are extrinsic, creative, group and group comparative.

Extrinsic:

1. I have been told that I help others grow and develop in their jobs.
7. I value and respect people who have different views and attitudes to my own.
23. We cannot rely on the present or the past, if we are going to be successful in the future.

Creative:

16. I put forward ideas, to which the group becomes committed.
32. I prefer ideas to facts or opinions.
44. I persuade others through creating a shared vision and understanding.
55. I paint an exciting picture of what could be rather than what is.

Group:

19. I persuade individuals in the group to share information.

34. Most decisions are taken by the team and not myself.
52. I focus on the goals of the group to persuade an individual member.
60. Teamworking is the way forward.

Group Comparative:

9. I prefer to work in a team rather than on my own.
26. Consensus is more effective than competition.
39. I prefer to work with the team rather than the individual.
46. I prefer to be part of group creativity sessions to thinking on my own.

Let us take three individuals with identical scores of 5. (Fooled you – you were anticipating two individuals with a score of 9!). The first answers the first and third extrinsic statement and the creative statements 16, 32 and 55 in the affirmative. The second answers the extrinsic questions in the affirmative, and statements 9 and 26 of group comparative. The third answers extrinsic statement 23, group statements 34 and 60, and group comparative statements 39 and 46.

The first score would support an ego persuader or individual strong in Logic and Incentives. A person with ideas and some visioning skills – but they are his ideas and vision, thrust on others. There is no ability to create a shared vision, nor unite the team behind that vision and drive forwards to effective change. The individual is not a team person nor is she empathetic.

You may have come across such individuals – your boss perhaps? I certainly have, as have many of the managers I have talked to. They give creativity a bad name, and strategic thinking as well – as some confuse being creative with being a strategic thinker.

I remember an executive I met on a senior executive programme I attended who was suffering severe withdrawal symptoms from one such boss. His boss worked on the twin principles 'an idea a day keeps the doctor away' and 'variety is the spice of life'. The poor executive and his henchmen ran around, like blue-arsed flies, trying to develop and implement ill-thought-out and mutually exclusive ideas mandated to them. The executive was a highly stressed heavy drinker, which should cause no surprise.

The second individual is likely to be strongly empathetic, without necessarily being either group orientated or creative. This explains the point made in Chapter 2 that a double dominance in Empathy and Group is a low probability. The strong carer is likely to be supported by a moderate G score – though creativity and group orientation are not impossible.

The third individual is group orientated, but neither creative nor necessarily comfortable with one-to-one relationships – perhaps a rather passive individual, a follower rather than a leader, who likes to hide in a crowd.

The foregoing, I hope, has brought to life the subtleties and variations that exist within each set of questions. As mentioned in Chapter 1 any individual providing a full counselling, coaching or support role would need to be aware of these variations and what they mean.

We now move on to the next chapter to examine the usefulness of the profile in the specific area of leadership.

4
◆ Leadership ◆

In this chapter we look at leadership and how the persuasion profile can give indications of the leadership approach we, as managers, adopt. We then move on to consider the traditional type of leader that has acted as a role-model for us, the kind of leadership required in the future, the current realities and issues that need to be addressed in the transition.

At the heart of leadership is the person – the personal qualities and skills the leader brings to her role, and how these are applied to the person or group of persons she is leading.

It is worth recording the findings of a survey, carried out by Management Centre Europe in 1988. More than 1,000 European managers were asked what they considered were the attributes of a successful business leader and whether their own managing director had the desired attributes. I have limited the results to those where the desired attribute was mentioned by more than three-quarters of the respondents so as to focus on the priorities.

	Desired (%)	Actual (%)
1. Able to build effective teams.	96	50
2. Knows how to listen.	93	44
3. Capable of making decisions on his own.	87	66
4. Knows how to retain good people.	86	39
5. Surrounds himself with the top people.	85	50
6. Energetic.	85	62
7. Innovative.	83	47
8. Visionary.	79	45
9. Has high ethical standards.	76	53

It is fascinating to note the desire for an externally focused leader (in persuasion terms) and the extent of the gap perceived in the Empathy style (listening) and the Group style (team building, innovation and vision).

Leadership concerns itself with people. Persuasion concerns itself with people. The way we persuade will have a major impact on the way we lead. Let us look again at the profile, but this time with four leadership styles entered, one for each quadrant.

Where do they come from and what do they mean?

THE PROFILE AND LEADERSHIP

Control

Logic and Incentives are ego styles. In the incentive style, we use our authority (if we have it) and the stick and the carrot to ensure discipline, to exercise control and produce performance. The deployment of logic (whether rational or prejudicial) reinforces and deepens the control we gain through using incentives. In terms of leadership, the combination indicates a control orientation.

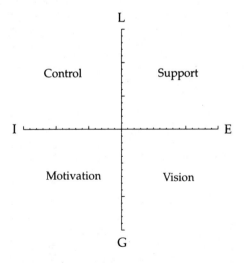

Figure 23 The leadership profile

Support

The empathy style is a highly supportive style though, as we have seen, it can indicate a lack of assertiveness. Instead of supporting, it becomes giving in. If bolstered by Logic and the ego position that represents, the support becomes effective. In leadership terms, I have called the combination support. Another possibility is a coaching orientation. As that tends to be seen as specific to work improvement (omitting general emotional support), and requires the application of specific skill that may be absent, I have stayed with the more general word, support.

Vision

The group style is a combination of creativity, vision and group focus. If supported by care and individual focus, it increases the leader's ability to unite the team (collectively and individually) behind a shared vision and goals. In leadership terms, I have called the combination, vision. It should be recognised that the control and support styles are basically one-to-one styles, and implicit in the word vision in this context is a strong group dimension.

Motivation

The incentives approach is based on a belief (often not consciously stated) that the stick and the carrot, supporting a controlled disciplined environment, will motivate. This can be the case, as many of us are motivated by financial and non-financial incentives or disincentives. Motivation is after all part of the definition of 'incentive'. Often their use by someone having little regard to our feelings, attitudes and personal goals significantly diminishes their impact.

However, when an external focus is added, with the emphasis on the group, and on generating common goals towards achieving a shared vision, the effectiveness of the motivational aspects increases. In leadership terms, I have called the combination, motivation. Again, in the context of a leadership style, there is an assumed group dimension.

As with the persuasion profile, clues as to leadership approaches are indicated by the combination of shape and size. In the UK and other cultures, both Western and African, there can be discerned a traditional, generic leadership approach. While there are both variations and different approaches, it is worth examining the traditional approach, its origins and implications.

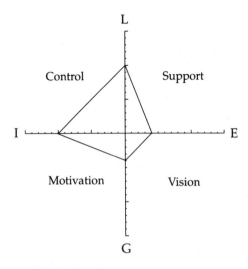

Figure 24 The traditional leader

TRADITIONAL

I have called the approach, command and control. The profile is set out in Figure 24 with scores (by way of example) of I = 10, L = 10, E = 4 and G = 4.

The preferences are in Logic and Incentives, with low scores in E and G. The gap of 6 between the I/L scores and the E/G scores implies that the preferred styles are the natural persuasion styles. The focus score of 12 means a strong internal focus.

In terms of leadership, the emphasis is on one-to-one relationships, with the leader seen and seeing himself as very much the man or woman in charge and in control.

Key aspects of the traditional leader and the traditional organisational setting in which he operated (and I use the masculine gender, as it is entirely appropriate) are set out below

Decisions

The leader took the decisions. It was his responsibility and duty, not to be shared with his followers (or subordinates – such a pejorative word). This was accepted. 'You're the boss, you decide'.

Hierarchy

The leader derived authority and power from his position in the hierarchy. He was formally placed above the follower, giving authority. He was provided with the power of appraisal, a considerable 'persuader'.

Control

The leader was the man in charge. He was the commander, leading from the front and in control of his troops. 'You are the boss.' The very word itself, in such common usage, defines the style!

Confrontation

Business was war – confrontation and competition. The battle was fought on all fronts, against the competitor, against the supplier, against other departments or functional/line areas, against his peers or rivals for promotion, and occasionally against the customer!

Reactive

While decision-taking was the leader's prerogative and not shared with the team, the area of decision-taking was very small. The leader reacted to commands from on high or responded to events perceived as outside his control. He and all his staff were usually rushed off their feet in a hive of reactive activity.

The command and control leader was the required leader for the business environment in which he operated. He functioned by and large in a predictable, ordered external environment. So structure, discipline, hierarchy, control were very appropriate. They generated order in an ordered world. The reactive command and control approach was required to ensure that order. Years of profitability were enjoyed as a result – with a few hiccups on the way.

It was also the cultural norm – the father of the family was the command and control role-model.

As we will see when we look at the transition, breaking free from this role and historic reality is very difficult. Before doing so, let us consider in which direction the change is heading and why. Let us consider the future leader.

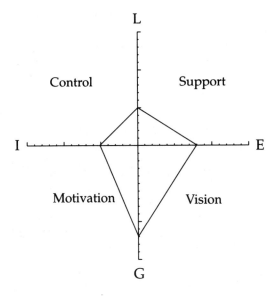

Figure 25 The VTL

FUTURE

I have called the future leader the Visionary Team Leader (VTL). You may recognise her by another name – the inspirer. The profile is set out in Figure 25.

The VTL is fundamentally group or team orientated, with well-developed creative and visionary skills, moderate scores in Logic and Incentives, with a moderate to strong external focus. The low Logic score does not imply incompetence in logical thinking, simply preference and ability elsewhere. The focus within Logic would be on the rational rather than the prejudicial or competitive. The focus in Incentives would be on motivation, performance and praise.

A key characteristic is the secondary in Empathy, supporting the dominance in Group. The dominant characteristics of his leadership approach are effective team building, listening and supporting, creativity and vision.

Let us compare the new with the old.

Decisions

Instead of taking the decision, the VTL creates the environment in which decisions can be made. The decisions are taken and agreed by the team as a whole. This enriches the quality of the decisions because of information-sharing and group creativity. It makes implementation much more effective, because of ownership of the decisions taken.

Teams

The hierarchy provides an individual focus, increasingly emphasised by individually based targets and bonuses. Where there are status differentials within a so-called team, effective teamworking becomes very difficult. The structure for VTL to be effective is much flatter, with a team and not an individual base. He will not need positional power and authority, but skill and respect. Additionally, the shift in leadership approach must be supported by a shift away from individual targets and bonuses to team targets and rewards.

Empowerment

No more the leader in control, but the leader who learns with, and empowers, her team. The VTL is the change agent who catalyses, harnesses and focuses the talents of the individual within the framework of the team.

Co-operation

War, cost-cutting, competition and confrontation are replaced by added value, co-operation and collaboration – joint ventures with 'competitors', cross-functional teams, co-operation within teams, and a relationship, nay partnership, with supplier and customer.

Proactive

The VTL is proactive, creative, and visionary not for himself but for the team, and not by himself but with the team.

This is a fundamental change, the implications of which will be examined in the section on Transition. But is this view, shared by many, a fantasy or future reality?

The external business world for many companies today and for most, if not all, to-morrow, is a complex, dynamic, ambiguous, risky, uncertain one. The definitions of, and entry barriers to, markets are crumbling under the forces of globalisation, de-regulation and technological change. Competition increases in breadth and depth. Power shifts to customers, as their choice and knowledge grows. Mergers, de-mergers, takeovers and bankruptcies beckon.

The fundamental shift is from controlling order to managing change or even riding the chariot of chaos.

The cry is to add value to customers. The means is to empower the employee. The leadership style is VTL.

After all, as the survey showed, visionary team leadership is the approach desired by the managers of today from the leaders of today. Perhaps they will make their dreams reality, as they are the leaders of tomorrow.

CURRENT REALITIES

Have we any clues as to the extent the traditional leader still holds sway, what are the current realities, and the implications?

Yes! Recent research gives us some interesting answers to current leadership styles at the top. Additionally, we have some useful findings as to the approach of middle management to leadership.

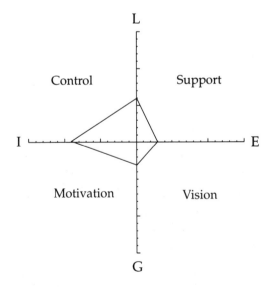

Figure 26 The oversensitive

Our managing directors

During 1990, Professor Andrew Kakabadse, a management development expert, conducted an exhaustive survey of British business covering more than 1,100 managers in 740 organisations. The purpose of the survey was to uncover the leadership style of the managing director (MD) and determine the effect on staff and performance.

I detail the six distinct styles uncovered, using the names the Professor used.

The oversensitive

Emotional, erratic, and easily wounded, they allow their mood to influence their judgement, take criticism personally and judge others on whether they are on the same wavelength rather than on their achievements. They blame themselves for others' mistakes and become drained and depressed.

Characteristics of the profile would be a low E score (not an empathetic individual), a low G score (neither a team nor a creative person), a moderate L score (of the emotional, prejudicial variety), and a preference in Incentives. The focus would be strongly internal, and the most developed and deployed leadership quadrant would be control.

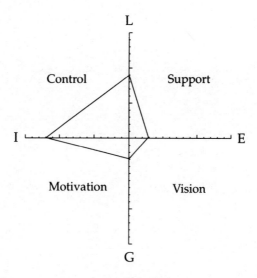

Figure 27 The disciplinarian

The disciplinarian

Sticklers for formality, rules and nit-picking, they believe rigorous discipline brings success. Though respected for efficiency, they are resented for inflexibility and abrasive manner.

Characteristics of the profile would be a dominance in Incentives, a secondary in Logic, with low E and G scores. There would be an even stronger internal focus than the oversensitive and, again, the dominant leadership quadrant is control.

This individual is very close indeed to the traditional leader we have already covered. Indeed, we will see that five out of the six approaches have much in common with that generic role-model.

Self-made man

Often owners of the companies they started, they believe that only they have the drive, ideas and charm to find success. They cannot delegate, and see the team as an extension of their ego.

Well, we have met this character before – the ego persuader or Maxwell lookalike. He is likely to have a double dominance in Incentives and Logic, a low E score, but a moderate G score, reflecting a degree of creativity and vision but no external team orientation.

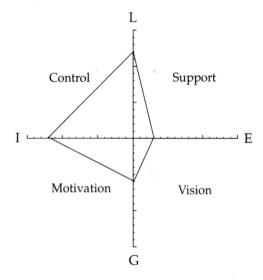

Figure 28 The self-made man

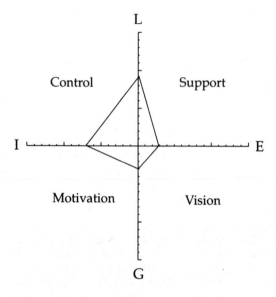

Figure 29 The secretive

The focus is excessively internal, and control comes out of this individual's ears!

The secretive

They communicate only on a need-to-know basis, feel awkward in a group, and limit the risk by saying little.

Considering the profile, I would suggest a low G score (yet again), a low E score, a preference in Logic (more of the factual than the competitive), and a moderate score in Incentives. As usual not a people person nor a team person, but not excessive in the use of incentives, relying more on positional power.

This is someone tailor-made for the ivory tower, with but a few less-than-trusted lieutenants, and no desire for the panoply of the full court. Control is less dominant than in the other cases, but is still his most significant leadership style. As regards focus, it is in the moderate range rather than strong or excessive.

The specialist

Proud of their expertise, they communicate easily with fellow

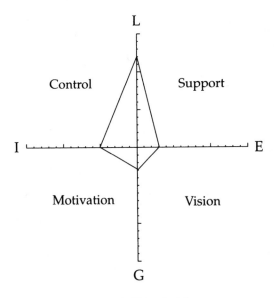

Figure 30 The specialist

specialists but not with others. Solutions to problems are theoretically accurate but often unworkable.

Well, we have met a close relative of this character before – the cold fish. He is likely to be dominant in Logic, with a low G score and E score, and a moderate score in Incentives. (The cold fish who has made leader is likely to have a moderate I score!).

Though the emphasis is different from the other species, the end result is similar – a large bias towards control as a leader. Yet again, a strong internal focus.

The integrator

The most successful type, they have a rare combination of abilities to recognise the needs of their staff, while keeping an eye on those of the customer. They take time to learn the business and reach agreement with staff on the way forward. Their staff are happy, open and disciplined.

Alas, the only one out of six – somewhere I fancy between our assertive persuader and our VTL. My suggested profile would be a moderate score in Incentives, and a triple preference in Logic, Empathy and Group. He would be the only type with an external focus, but only in the weak range. He is probably not a strong,

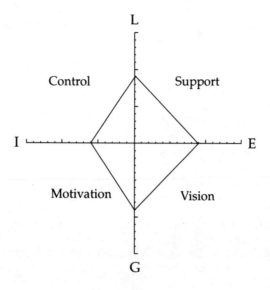

Figure 31 The integrator

creative visionary. It is that development that moves the Group
from strong into dominant, and Logic from strong to moderate.

The Integrator of today will become the VTL of tomorrow.

Two points before we move on to look at the manager, rather
than the MD.

1. If we ignore the one successful type, who is in a significant
   minority, the other five are characterised by the following
   features:
   — The primary leadership style is to exercise control, rather
      than to support or to provide vision, direction, and
      motivation.
   — They are internally focused. They are 'I' leaders rather than
      'You and I' or 'We' leaders.
   — They focus on one-to-one relationships and not on develop-
      ing group relationships.
   — They are logically developed but emotionally and (bar one
      type) creatively retarded. This is to be expected.

   MDs of today will, on average, be over fifty. Their
   leadership role-model is command and control, whether it
   was their own fathers or other people's fathers who led
   them in their formative business years. They were educated

into Logic and Incentives, and received no explicit education in creativity or how to manage relationships. Finally,
the vast majority will not have had any subsequent training
in leadership skills.

2. European managers want a VTL for their MDs. Some of the
respondents would have been British managers. Assuming
that British managers, as a whole, want a VTL, the implication
of the above results is the gap between desired and actual is
even greater for the UK than elsewhere in Europe. This is a
matter of some concern, given 1992 and beyond.

Our managers

Now, I have been privileged to train many managers in leadership.
Additionally, Sundridge Park Management Centre has built up a
database on leadership styles. In this section, I want to focus on
current styles, as well as the implications of the historic role-model.
Before doing so, I want to make a few points on roles, an approach
pioneered by Peter Drucker.

It is very helpful to put our work activities and skills deployed
(and for that matter non-work activities and skills deployed) into
a role context.

We can think of the manager through to senior executive or even

ROLE MIX

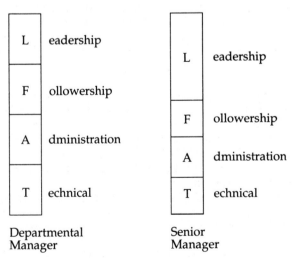

Figure 32 Role mix

managing director as carrying out a number of roles. In fact, exactly the same roles are carried out, but in different proportions, depending on position in the company. Figure 32 exemplifies the roles and mix for a manager, and the senior manager. There are four roles.

Leadership

Whether supervisor, junior manager, departmental manger or senior manager, we have a responsibility and a duty to lead those we are put in charge of. The nature of that leadership role is a matter of intense debate among academics, gurus and some practitioners. But for many in a leadership role – and that role starts as soon as we are in a position of authority over another member of staff – there is no debate, because the role is not recognised.

The fact that we may not think of ourselves as leaders nor have training in leadership simply means that the blind lead the blind. Our focus may be on the job and not the person. Our focus may be on ourselves and not the follower. Nevertheless we provide, without thought and control, a pattern of behaviour and approach subconsciously that sets boundaries on the performance and motivation of those we are not consciously leading.

It is either the absence of recognition of this crucial leadership role or the absence of any training and support to enable us to carry it out effectively (if the role is recognised) that leads to incompetence and to the continuation of worst practise.

We are in such a role when, at the most fundamental level, we talk to a 'subordinate', never mind chair a meeting of subordinates or appraise a subordinate or praise a subordinate and so on.

Followership

We are also followers or in a subordinate role. Even the managing director has such a role, when he reports to the board.

If leadership training is scarce, then followership training is non-existent. We learn how to be a follower by absorbing the culture and modifying our behaviour, depending on our understanding, interest and political skill, according to the unwritten rules we pick up along the way.

It is fortunate indeed that the skills of an effective follower are very similar to those of an effective leader. For those interested in this reality, I would refer you to the excellent *Harvard Review Business* article published in the November–December 1988 edition by Robert E Kelley, entitled 'In praise of followers'.

We carry out the followership role, whenever we interact with our boss or more senior staff, whenever we attend a meeting as a team-member and so on.

Technical

The technical role is when we carry out activities that relate to our professional competence, whether as a lawyer, an architect, a consultant, a product manger, a production manager, a marketeer, a salesman, a strategic planner, an IT manager, and so on.

It is the role which is often perceived as the most important role, both by the corporate culture and by the individual manager. The combination of focus on the technical role and the absence of training in the leadership role explains why so many managers are poor delegators, and work very long hours to less than optimum effect.

Administration

The final role is self-explanatory. Our working lives are full of administration matters. We have to organise ourselves (with or without IT support) and deal with the volumes of paper that result from being part of an organisation.

The usefulness of thinking in terms of such roles (and we are likely to carry out all the roles more than once in one working day) is:

■ We can identify the skills requirements of each role, the degree of overlap and the degree of separation. We can devise and implement a plan to maximise our competence in each role. The lack of separation into roles has, as we have seen, reduced the perception of importance of the 'soft' roles of leadership and followership and over-emphasised the importance of the 'hard' roles of technical and administration – with a severe reduction in personal and corporate effectiveness as a result.
■ We can identify which work activity slots into which role, and therefore apply the appropriate skill or competence to that activity. How often have we left a meeting as a follower, feeling very frustrated or angry and then taken it out on one of our own followers, only to regret and apologise. If we were more effective followers, we might not be so frustrated. Even if we were, but consciously recognised the switch in roles, we might have tempered our approach to our own follower.

Now let us turn to current styles of leadership among managers, with apologies for the long delay, and in the hope that you perceived the digression as valuable.

Current styles

A widely used instrument on leadership programmes is called Situational Leadership devised by Kenneth Blanchard, Ronald Hambleton, Douglas Forsyth and Drea Zigarni. The individual is presented with 20 different leadership situations and has to select one of four alternative approaches for each situation.

The subsequent analysis indicates the preferred style, the secondary style and the style(s) that needs development. The instrument also indicates both how flexible and effective her leadership approach is.

Each style represents a combination of a control approach and a supportive approach. As we would expect, the control approach reflects a task orientation and directive behaviour and the support approach a people orientation, and supportive behaviour.

There are four combinations or styles:

- S1: High directive and low supportive behaviour.
- S2: High directive and high supportive behaviour.
- S3: Low directive and high supportive behaviour.
- S4: Low directive and low supportive behaviour.

For this instrument, there is an optimal outcome. This is an equal score of five in each style, which gives 100 per cent flexibility. Choosing the style, which matches the nature of the situation and maturity of the follower gives 100 per cent effectiveness.

The instrument does not give a group perspective, nor does it concern itself with vision or motivation.

The actual results for hundreds of middle managers are a very low preference for S1 (and when it occurs it tends to be in front-line manufacturing!), a very low preference for S4, a majority preferring S3 (with S2 as the support), and a significant minority preferring S2 (with S3 as the support).

So what? What this tells us is that while managing directors are still locked into control styles, their middle managers in the age range 25 to 40 are moving from control towards support, retaining control as a secondary. In terms of our profile, the move is from traditional command and control with a strong ego focus through control and support with a weak ego focus to support with control and a neutral focus. These three profiles are set out in Figures 33, 34 and 35.

The reasons for this shift are not too difficult to uncover. They are fivefold.

- If we start with the family, the nuclear family of husband, wife and 2.2 children is increasingly less and less the norm. Women,

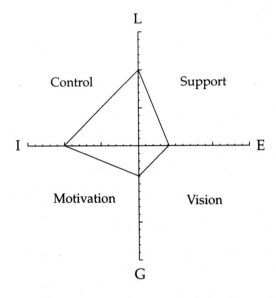

Figure 33 Leadership styles: command and control

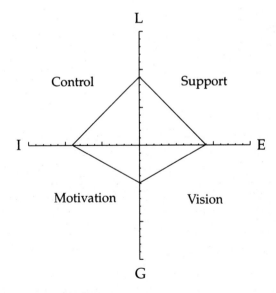

Figure 34 Leadership styles: control and support

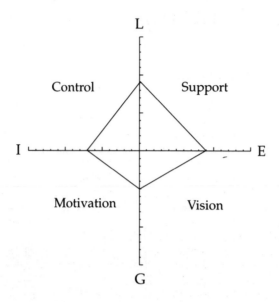

Figure 35 Leadership styles: support with control

the predominant single parent, have a natural disposition to support rather than command. Additionally, the father, when role-model, is no longer providing command and control as a natural style, but a much more supportive and open approach.

■ Unlike their senior managers, these managers have, in increasing numbers, undertaken some form of management training.

■ There is a reaction to the leadership style (and its variations) received from on high. There is no longer an automatic transference downwards, as managers question its wisdom. They recognise from their own reactions and experience the shortcomings of the style, and how demotivating and frustrating it is for them.

■ Many are in the middle of fundamental change and uncertainty, and have recognised that a supportive approach to their own followers is critical to their own success in managing change.

■ Their followers are becoming more assertive and demanding, and less tolerant of the arid command and control approach.

I deal with the implications in the final section on the Transition, having first looked at the impact of the command and control style, and the organisational context.

THE TRANSITION

Impact of command and control

I have already covered how the managers of today are moving towards support, and away from control, though retaining a control aspect. In any period of transition, there will be continuity with the past, unless there is fundamental exogenous shock.

Unfortunately, there is no focus and direction to the change. It is a reactive change (and I have mentioned the five forces influencing the change) not a proactive managed change. This makes the birth of the VTL difficult and slow, if it occurs. We may yield to competitors from other cultures, where the base is not so low, and the pace of change faster and more directed.

What I have noticed is that power of the traditional view of the leader is very strong. During our leadership programmes, we run outdoor activities, focused on problem solving. In each team, everyone has the opportunity to lead and to observe. The leadership effectiveness is often high – and the leader feels guilty. She has been effective by taking on a co-ordinating role and not a command role, or allowing the leadership to pass elsewhere, or being mainly detached and observing the activities of the rest of the team, intervening constructively where necessary. As we say, 'getting into the helicopter' so that she can see the wood for the trees, when everyone else is deep in the forest of activity.

Often in the feedback session immediately afterwards (by far the most valuable part of the process), I have heard comments from the leader along the lines of:

'I was a very bad leader, because I was not in charge', to which the group responds 'Oh! no, you weren't!'
'I wanted to take control, but I felt it wouldn't be appropriate.'

And slowly, through the reality of experience, perceptions and attitudes begin to change, with often a longing glance backwards: 'Well, of course, it would be different back at work. Here, I have no formal authority over the team. In any case, they are peers, and not subordinates.' To which we say: 'Oh! No, it shouldn't (be different).'

The point is that the traditional role-model casts a long shadow over effective change. We need to change the model, if we are going to change the leader.

Organisational approaches

From one perspective, an organisation is but the sum of the people working for it. Those with the most power to effect change are those in positions of greatest authority.

Managers, who do not recognise that they have a critical leadership role or do not acquire the skills to carry it out effectively do not lead effectively by default. Senior managers and directors who do not recognise they have a critical role as change-masters or do not acquire skills to be change-masters fail to manage change effectively by default.

So client-first schemes, which become staff-second realities, do not work. Quality standards like BS5750, ISO9000 or TQM programmes, addressing processes and not people will not work. Removing management layers without IT and training support will fail. Changing structures but not hearts and minds will not be sufficient.

There is, alas, no shared vision and common goals. There is no awareness that training is an organisational imperative, not just an individual need.

There are also many individual examples of progress on the back of understanding. For instance, one company I have heard of is introducing assessment from below, one way of enforcing a change in leadership approach!

One division of a large financial services company I know is trying to grasp the nettle. The findings of an external consultancy report were internalised – the best way.

Before, the division was organised on product lines with hierarchical teams and traditional leaders. Now, extremely rapidly, they are reorganising on customer lines with flat cross-product teams. The training manager recognises the need for training in team leadership, teamworking and team building. But there is a recession, there is a budget, and there are traditional leaders in positions of power.

Success or failure is not dependent on the structural changes, perceived as vital but on the people changes. The same people who were command and control merchants have to become VTLs or at least team leaders. The same people who were non-assertive followers have to become either effective followers or newly appointed team leaders. What is required is a rapid effective training programme that achieves critical mass in a relatively short time.

The jury is out. It is ironic that the power of success or failure to a large extent depends on the networking and persuasion skills of one middle manager. It is why persuasion is so important a skill.

If change-masters don't do their job, the middle manager has to.

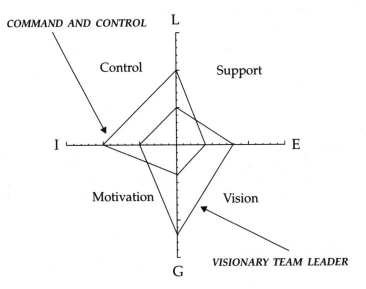

Figure 36 Summary profile: traditional and VTL

IMPLICATIONS

Finally, I want to look specifically at the individual manager as leader, and highlight the implications of the change from command and control to VTL. Figure 36 is a summary profile that shows the traditional command and control role-model and the suggested new role-model – the VTL.

Looking at each quadrant, we have:

Control

There is a fundamental shift away from the focus on Incentives and Logic. The reduction in Incentives would be concentrated in the control and discipline areas. With developing Empathy and Group skills, the competitive and comparative aspects of Logic would diminish and the rational aspects come to the fore.

Support

The key feature is the significant increase in Empathy, but this would not be in the subdominant category. The move is away from the aggressive approach that is implied by a strong command and control leadership style to an assertive approach, but certainly not a submissive one.

Vision

This is the key move – the unlocking of the creative side of the brain (which we all have) and the development of a team focus and skills.

Motivation

There is a switch away from a reliance on incentives on an individual basis towards a sharing of goals – agreeing rather then setting objectives in the context of the team's needs.

'Oh! Yes!' I hear you say. 'That is a bit of a tall order, assuming I agree with some aspects of the nature and direction of change. And another thing. We seem to have moved somewhat from me as a persuader, and how I can become more effective.'

Point taken. There is much common ground between being more effective as a leader, and more effective as a persuador – namely (for many) being more developed in the Empathy and Group approaches for both group and individual interactions.

So, in the next chapters, we look at improving individual and group skills before examining the persuasion situation, where the interaction is one on one.

5

◆ Listening ◆

INTRODUCTION

Before moving forward, let us take stock.

You have completed the ILEG Inventory, and produced your profile. You may have also produced the profile which reflects another's perception of how you persuade. Through this process, and by reading the subsequent chapters on what each persuasion approach means and what the combinations, relative strengths and focus mean, you should have gained a clearer perception of where you are in persuasion terms and why you persuade as you do.

You may well recognise and appreciate particular strengths in your approach as well as uncovering areas where further development would improve your effectiveness.

You have also seen how the Inventory results provide a perspective on your leadership style, as well as considering how leadership styles as a whole are shifting as the external business environment changes radically and rapidly.

Finally, you have been introduced to two role-models – the assertive persuader in the one-to-one situation and the VTL in the group situation.

In the next four chapters, we concentrate on examining the key skills that will enable us to be more effective, first as assertive persuaders and then as VTLs.

Let me remind you of the assertive persuader's profile.

The persuasion preferences are Logic and Empathy. The emphasis in Logic would be rational and factual rather than being prejudicial or competitive. The emphasis in Empathy would be listening and assertive. Additionally the assertive persuador would have well-developed questioning skills so that she can establish the emotional and knowledge base of the persuadee.

So we will look at the art of listening in this chapter, and in the next, the science of questioning and the assertive approach.

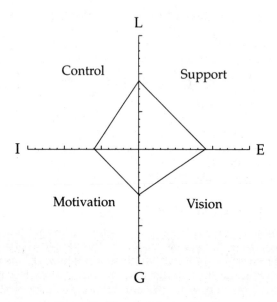

Figure 37 The assertive persuader

LISTENING

There are four questions we will address:

- Why is listening important?
- Why is listening difficult?
- How we can identify poor listening?
- How can we become better listeners?

Before we start, time for a true story. I have a colleague, an Associate of Sundridge Park Management Centre, who runs the outdoor activities on our leadership programmes. He is very competent and effective. He is not ex-SAS, nor a command and control merchant. He is quietly spoken, and one of his favourite questions to the delegates during the activities is: 'Have you got your ears on?'

Now, at the beginning, quite a number of the managers have not got their ears on. By the end, nearly all have.

Why?

Few managers I have met welcome failure. More importantly, as team cohesion inevitably grows, they desire more not to fail for the team than for themselves. If they don't listen, they can't succeed.

It is a lesson well learnt. They have changed their definition of what is important. We will be more effective listeners if we try to listen because we consider either the individual or the content important. Similarly, we are more creative if we spend more time thinking, because we have decided thinking time is important.

A change in attitude provides the base to improvement. Learning and understanding techniques are the building blocks. Developing skill through the application of techniques in practice completes the structure. Each component is required in the right order for complete success.

Why is listening important?

If we become effective listeners, we will improve our competence as persuaders. As covered already, listening is at the heart of becoming an assertive persuader, producing the marvellous win/win outcomes that are good for us as persuaders, good for the persuadees, often our 'subordinates', and good for the companies we serve.

Whatever the corporate culture, assertive persuaders flourish.

Moreover, effective listening improves our competence in a whole host of management activities, such as interviewing, negotiating, selling, coaching, appraising and so on.

In short, effective listening enhances our competence in any situation, involving communication with others.

Why is listening difficult?

Research has shown that managers are 50 per cent less effective at listening than they think they are. Equally, the research into the attributes desired from a managing director by their managers had 'knows how to listen' as the second most important (desired by 93 per cent) with the 'actual' figure one of the lowest at 44 per cent. In fact, the gap of 49 per cent between desired and actual is the highest!

So listening skills are important, desired, but often absent. There are six reasons why listening is difficult.

Talkers are rewarded

If we go back to our upbringing, to beyond conscious memory (and to the preface of this book!), we learnt as babies that making a noise brought attention and satisfaction. As children, the noisiest and loudest often became the leaders and innovators of childhood games and activities. In formal education, those children who always answered questions and spoke out clearly and distinctly were more favoured and praised.

In adult and business life the pattern continues. Those who make the most noise often gain more attention than they or their opinions deserve.

The talkers are rewarded.

While we need to learn to speak well and effectively – to assert our views and opinions, there is a cultural imbalance. Listening can be seen as passive, as indicating a submissive stance – suggesting we have nothing to say. Listening loses the limelight.

The above has validity but suggests a dichotomy – either we are talkers or we are listeners. The assertive persuader avoids such polarisation. She talks when it is appropriate and listens when it is appropriate. The assertive persuader is proactive like an effective leader or an effective follower – in control of the situation but not in command of the persuadee.

We are more important

We have touched on this already. Many of us are strong in the ego styles, and there is no balance in Empathy or Group. We say to ourselves, though not often at the conscious level, that we are more important than the persuadee. If we happen to be the 'boss' of the persuadee, that view will be reinforced by our positional power and perceived status.

We cannot begin to listen effectively unless we are prepared to make what can be a fundamental change in attitude. We must recognise and appreciate that the persuadee has a potentially positive contribution to make. We must recognise that we have the responsibility as persuader to change the potential to actual through our effective listening and questioning skills.

Let us return to the learning ladder. At the lowest level we do not appreciate that we are not as effective listeners/persuaders as we think. If we gain the conscious perception of lack of competence, then it is not that difficult, once techniques are absorbed, for us to consciously improve our competence by structured practice over time (see final chapter on Planning to Improve). Eventually we become competent without having to think about it.

If we think about our driving, the perception of the need to drive was there (perhaps before the age of seventeen!), we received instruction in techniques, and after much practice, we drove without thinking. However, we can get into bad habits – so we occasionally need to 'get into the helicopter' and propel ourselves back to the conscious levels in the learning ladder – revisit the techniques, consciously improve our competence, then rest a while in blissful competence! The process is iterative over time.

We are the experts

A little knowledge is a dangerous thing. A lot of knowledge can be even more dangerous, when it comes to listening. It is a variation of the perception of importance theme – but this time it is not a perception that the individual is not important, but that what he has to say – the content – is not important. We are the experts. We say to ourselves, deep down, 'Those who know nothing have nothing to say'. Innocence and ignorance can be the source of much creativity and subsequent knowledge. However, most of us succumb, individually and collectively to the 'new boy syndrome'. 'Until you have earned your spurs, proved your competence, you have nothing to say'. Many inventions have occurred because someone did not know 'it couldn't be done', and somebody else listened!

It reminds me of one highlight of my training experience. As part of team-building, we use instruments that measure synergy. One is called 'The sub-Antarctic survival situation'. Each individual has to decide the order of importance to her survival of a number of items left over from the crash of a plane, leaving her and some colleagues alive.

The decision-making process is then repeated, but this time by a group of individuals. By comparing the team rankings and the individual rankings with the expert rankings (provided at the end), the gain or loss of the team score compared with the average of the individual scores can be determined. The extent of the gain is a measure of the value gained or synergy of the group compared to the individuals.

For the participants, it is a very stimulating, often amusing and powerful learning experience. Invariably, one of the lessons is the importance and value to be gained from listening in the group situation.

Now I have administered this session many times. There have been many different results, almost invariably some synergy and, occasionally, a remarkable degree of synergy, reflecting the appropriate attitudes, behaviours and skills required. Not very often, there is 'negative synergy' and once, only once, there was very negative synergy! In other words, all of the individuals in the group would have had a greater chance of avoiding death by operating on their own.

As is often the case, I remember the failure with far greater clarity than the success – partly because of the failure itself, and partly because I knew I would have to pick up the emotional pieces.

The reason for this spectacular result was the presence in a group of five of not one but two experts. Well, they were relative experts. They had not actually crash-landed in the sub-Antarctic, but they had both travelled extensively and enjoyed solo journeys in rough terrain. So they were experts relative to the other three.

Half the allotted time of 45 minutes was devoted to the clash of the titans, who agreed on absolutely nothing. The other three were completely ignored and silent. Eventually, the sole woman in the group had had enough and very assertively and effectively parted the protagonists. Some semblance of reasonable debate commenced, but the clock ran out, and a rush of ill-considered choices was made.

Some strong messages were passed in the debrief by the woman and her other colleagues to these experts, and many of these were eventually absorbed and acted upon, as the group performance and cohesion grew. (The most effective transfer and receipt of messages comes when a group has developed a cohesion, a mutual respect among the individual members and the comments are made in a positive, constructive and assertive manner by one to the other in the context of open group debate. That is the highest level. Tutors, operating in a facilitating role, drawing out the messages and encouraging understanding and ownership is less powerful, but a necessary precursor).

We think faster than we speak

This means that, as listeners, we have time available, which can either be put to good use by concentrating and trying to fully comprehend what is being said to us or to bad use by allowing distractions and our own thoughts to intrude.

Our mind-sets

From the moment of our birth, we enter an uncertain world, with a complexity and a dynamic that we can never comprehend. We are therefore driven, whether consciously or not, to manage that uncertainty. Some of us are capable of tolerating, even enjoying high levels of ambiguity and uncertainty, but for all of us there is a degree and intensity that is unbearable.

To enable us to cope, we create and confirm areas of certainty – beliefs, assumptions, attitudes and opinions that we do not consciously question. If we did, we would raise the level of uncertainty in our lives. We would be taking a risk, as we do not know what is the breaking point for us.

Our minds become set.

There is, as always, a balance required. These areas of certainty, the product of past experiments and experience, help us to understand the present situation and the persuadee. However, they can also lead to pre-judgement, to hasty conclusions – to hearing what we want to hear, and not what the persuadee wants us to hear.

We can be poor speakers

The fault does not always lie with the listener. We can be poor speakers. We can speak too quickly. We can send out too much information. We can send veiled messages with unsuitable language and speech patterns or mixed messages using body language inconsistent with the words we speak.

How can we identify poor listening?

If we can identify poor listening in ourselves, we can then improve. If we identify poor listening in others, then we can attempt to rectify the situation. It is the function of an assertive persuader not only to listen effectively to the messages he receives from the persuadee, but also ensure that the messages he transmits are picked up by the persuadee.

At the heart of poor listening is body language – the non-verbal signals transmitted – the gestures we make or postures we take up. But language also has a part to play. There are six useful classifications:

Aggressive listening

Deliberate: We don't want to listen, but we have been forced to listen, perhaps by a direct, emotional request, and we have responded aggressively. Our heart is not in it, and we feel resentful at 'being forced to listen'. We fold our arms, presenting a barrier to the receipt of information, have a stiff posture and tend to glare.

Accidental: There is another type of aggressive listening, which is unintentional. We feel we ought to be listening, but aren't very skilled, and we try too hard. Because we are not listening effectively, we feel the need to verbally reassure the persuadee that we are. Our concentration at the conscious level leads us to leaning forward (perhaps invading the persuadee's personal body space unintentionally) with a rather stiff posture. What we think is an interested look from us is perceived as a discomforting stare by the persuadee.

Passive listening

A very common form of poor listening! This is when we have no strong desire to speak, have resigned ourselves to listen (perhaps we are with a person who likes to hear the sound of her voice) and we drift off slumped in the chair, body half-turned away from the speaker, hand over mouth to conceal the occasional yawn, and little eye contact as we tend to look elsewhere.

Listening Interruptus

This is where we don't want to listen, we want to speak. In the early stages (assuming we cannot find an appropriate moment to interrupt), we are likely to fidget in some fashion, such as drumming our fingers or playing with a pencil (assuming that is not the way we display nerves, when speaking). Then we lean forward, and interrupt.

We do a lot of videoed role-plays on our programmes. Occasionally, both the persuader and persuadee are in this mode simultaneously. The result is a bewildering dance of never completed statements or themes, as the talking prize is snatched one from the other, and back again. The bodies move forward when talking and back as the threatened invasion of personal body space forces the involuntary move. The occasional fidget manifests itself if the unnatural state of silence is too prolonged!

Logical listening

This is where we listen with our minds, but not our hearts. We are deaf to the messages conveyed by the way the persuadee speaks the words, and the non-verbal signals provided. We hear and respond to the words only. 'I've got a headache.' 'Then take an aspirin!'

Logical listening is often the precursor to passive listening. We start semi-detached because we are operating only at the logical and not emotional level. We are quick with the obvious logical solutions, become bored and lapse into passive listening.

Logical listening can also be the precursor to aggressive listening. The persuadee wants to share the feelings behind the verbal messages she makes, and is quite capable of working out the logical responses for herself. She picks up the lack of eye contact, the lack of warm, supportive body language, as well as the irritation provided by the statement of the obvious. Assuming the conversation is not terminated, she will often make an emotional appeal. 'You are just not listening to me.'

We, as persuaders, often respond to the emotional message, too clear to ignore, in a knee-jerk, emotionally negative way - aggressive listening. To avoid this, we have to take a deep, conscious breath and recognise the trap we have set for ourselves, before we fall in.

Arrogant listening

When we feel very comfortable and confident, often in front of a subordinate, we can adopt this posture – hands clasped behind our heads, as leaning back, legs stretched forward or even on the desk, as we gaze at the ceiling or down our noses! It does not necessarily display arrogance when we are on our own, as we could just be thinking. But it does if we are with another person, and we are supposed to be listening.

It's a posture that many of us adopt very frequently. In fact, quite a few managers reject the arrogant undertones when I point them out. But it is interesting to note how we automatically remove our feet from the desk, and change our stance, when the boss comes in! Also, in some oriental countries, where the cult of the individual is less strong, it causes personal affront and it is a cultural no-no ever to display the soles of the feet to a business colleague or acquaintance.

It is an ego-based style of listening, based on the assumption of superiority over the persuadee, and is very passive in the sense of complete disinterest at both the logical and emotional levels. The body language is static, as the posture will be maintained whether we talk or 'listen'. There is no positive eye contact, although we do not mind 'looking down our noses' at the persuadee, the only way we can look in that position!

If our attention is eventually caught, then we will alter our posture and gestures, depending on whether we move into logical listening, aggressive listening or listening interruptus. If we take that deep breath, recognise what we are doing and why, we can move into effective listening.

Nervous listening

There is one other form of listening which we can manifest when we are in an awkward situation – a job interview, appraisal interview with ego-persuader boss, trying to persuade a difficult boss or client and so on.

We want to listen, we try to listen, but we are only capable of listening to our heart beat. This form of non-listening manifests itself by nervous gestures, which can also be displayed when we have to talk. There are almost an infinite number of nervous gestures, and each person has a favourite. The point is that we usually do not know that we are making them. It is a matter of great surprise to managers, when they see themselves on video for the first time, to recognise this reality. We fiddle with our fingers, we fiddle with our hair, we fiddle with our faces. We cover our mouths and move the forefinger up and down our top lips, we tap-dance under the table, we move our chairs and tickle our ears. The list goes on and on.

I remember washing my face at night, and seeing a dark smudge on my right forehead. For years, I never could work out why it was there. Then I became interested in and more aware of body language, as part of the learning curve of a trainer – and I saw myself on video.

I smoke a pipe, and often push down the tobacco with the top of my right forefinger. I do this sometimes when I re-light a half-smoked pipe. Later, when nervous, I rub the top right of my forehead with the same digit – and hey presto!

I should say I used to. I have, by an effort, eradicated that gesture. Unfortunately, I have now joined the hand over mouth and top lip brigade! Not unfortunately, but fortunately, as I tend to catch myself out now, as it is a more visible gesture. Of course, we cannot easily control nervous gestures – they are nature's way of telling an observant persuadee that we are nervous. If we cease, it means we are no longer nervous.

As an aside, developing the ability to notice another's involuntary gestures and hence nervousness is a useful skill. If we want empathy, we know we have a lot of work to do. If there has been verbal agreement to something we have said, we know that it was involuntary agreement, unlikely to transfer into action.

As nervous listeners, there is little we can do, except take that deep breath, or breaths, to calm ourselves. Our nervous listening will also be conveyed by the fact we ask for information to be repeated, because we have not heard it properly, or by coming in with the answer to the wrong question!

When it is the persuadee behaving in this annoying manner, remember he may just be nervous, and try to calm him rather than berate him.

A final point is that often we try to control our nerves and our gestures, and partially succeed. Assuming we are sitting down, the gestures move to our feet (the tap-dance or shuffle), which often cannot be seen. What a keen observer will notice is that we adopt a very rigid posture above the table!

How can we become better listeners?

There are a number of key steps that we can take to become better listeners.

Be committed

We have to want to become better listeners, and recognise the power of effective listening. Poor listening can destroy the speaker's confidence in her ability to communicate. This is especially true when people are clearly upset, inexperienced or junior in status. In the persuasion situation, that will be the outcome an ego persuader wants, and will achieve. Do we want that? Or do we want the power from relationship enhancement, the power from assertive persuasion, the power of that win/win outcome?

Unless we are committed to improving our listening ability, then we won't.

Be objective

We need to think, to take that deep breath and make that deliberate pause. As we have seen, it is our feelings, our opinions, our prejudices (whether against the person or the content) or our nerves which deny us effective listening.

Just as good leaders learn how to take control, not of others, but of themselves, so too does the effective listener. Taking the time out as a discussion starts to say to ourselves 'I am going to listen' will improve our skill. Deliberately pausing when that comment comes which will trigger an instant negative logical or emotional response will improve our skill. In short being proactive not reactive. That is not to say we do not reply the way we instantly want to reply – we simply pause deliberately to give ourselves the option.

We listen to ourselves so that we can listen better to another.

Appreciate silence

We tend to dislike silence, and rush in verbally to fill it. In fact, silence can be a very powerful way to uncover truth. At a judicious moment, when we have asked a searching question and received a short unsatisfactory response, or we have made a telling statement, we fall silent until the persuadee speaks. What will often happen is that the persuadee will reveal what she has tried to keep concealed.

She rushes in to fill that awkward pause. She is very consciously concerned at the silence. She is emotionally distracted, and what she was trying to consciously conceal slips out, or at the least a veil is removed.

However this reality has more to do with effective interviewing skills than with effective listening skills. The main point is that a natural discomfort with silence may often impair our effective listening, either because we do not pause to collect our thoughts and give a measured response, or we speak when it would have been better from the persuadee's point of view if we had remained silent. We can, by being silent, give the persuadee time to control emotions or gather thoughts, or simply share together a pleasant mood or ambience.

As Mozart said: 'Silence is the most profound sound in music.'

Use positive body language

The words we speak have only around 10 per cent of the total impact in face-to-face communication. The way we speak – the tones, modulation, intensity, phrasing and use of pauses – has around 35 per cent of total impact, and our body language – our gestures, posture and facial expression – a highly significant 55 per cent.

If we are listening empathetically, then we will display the right body language. If we consciously try to use the right body language, we will probably feel bloody awkward, but we will be better listeners – and conscious competence will lead over time to natural ability. A load of rubbish, I hear you say. Not at all. It is why people being trained in good telephone technique are told to smile. When they do, the tone of the voice becomes warmer, and this is picked up at the other end of the phone.

So let us consider facial expression, gestures and posture.

Facial expression: The facial expressions should reflect the feelings being expressed. If the persuader is feeling sad, look sad, if happy, look happy, and if angry, look angry – angry together against the source of the persuadee's anger.

If you are the source of anger, that's a different kettle of fish. If the persuadee is angry with you, and you look angry, then the persuadee will get the message that you are angry with him. In all probability, he will not be deceived. This the moment for the assertive pause, not the angry response.

If there are no emotions being expressed, as the persuadee is in logical mode, then look confident and thoughtful – you are both in thinking mode together.

There should be fairly frequent eye-contact, but never a glare nor a stare. This avoids looking out of the window (!), and conveys the message that you are, in fact, all ears.

Gestures: Gestures are for the speaker, not the listener. Through using appropriate gestures, the impact of the message conveyed is significantly enhanced. Gestures from the listener act as a distraction – a form of non-verbal interruption.

Posture: Now, there is not a single right posture, as the posture will vary according to the situation – the logic or emotion conveyed. However, in all situations an assertive posture should be used rather than an aggressive or submissive one. For instance, when seated, the persuader could take up an open position (neither legs nor arms folded), lean forward slightly, with the head a little to one side, and hands clasped loosely together, resting on the lap.

There are variations, such as leaning back slightly (to accommodate the other person leaning forward), open posture, with one hand on the chin and the other hand supporting the elbow or sitting straight with legs slightly apart, each hand resting on the appropriate knee – the Pharoah's position.

Another way of approaching effective postures is to consciously avoid all the postures we have covered under poor listening!

Use words

An effective listener uses words in the right tone to convey the right meaning. There are two aspects, reflection and interest.

Reflection: As we have seen, we should use our faces to reflect the speaker's feelings. Equally the words and tone can support this by paraphrasing the words or reflecting the feeling of the speaker. In the exchanges below, S stands for speaker, and L for listener.

S: I fell off my bike coming round a sharp bend.

L: Fell off your bike! That must have been upsetting.

S: The customer was delighted that I got him the full refund so quickly.

L: So would I have been, if I had been the customer.

Interest: Show interest by those little verbal noises or even words. The murmur 'mmmmhuh' (or variations, which I will not try to spell!) or 'Well, I never', 'You don't say' or combinations.

Ask questions

A good listener is a good questioner, the subject of the next chapter. Effective questioning will draw out the whole story, or uncover the underlying assumption or prejudice, or pick out the bone of contention.

Plan

We may want to improve our listening skills as persuader or persuadee. We may understand the techniques. But if we want to make real progress, we have to practise. If we want to practise effectively and efficiently, we have to implement a sound plan. We have to know when we have tried to listen, how often we tried and how well. We have to set targets and measure success over time.

It can be done. Over a year ago, a particular manager (let us call him James) attended our leadership in management programme. James was a cocky and over-confident young man, with a conceit of his own abilities. He was concealing subconscious insecurity. During the programme, his performance was visibly poor, even to him as well as his fellow delegates. Fortunately they were supportive in both the team and individual context.

On the last morning, when action plans were being written up, and there was time for a private chat, James was very open. He said that he had recognised that he had a problem. He was a poor listener. Specifically, he could not take criticism. If any individual criticised him, then that was that. He ignored them, as far as possible, and just would not listen to them. He only listened to those who praised him.

Together we devised a listening action plan. This was not to be shared with his boss, as was the norm – it was his personal private plan. We devised another one in another area to satisfy that requirement. Months later, he telephoned me, and we had another chat. I did all the listening, as he had all the news – good news.

The final chapter of this book, therefore, is devoted to Planning to Improve so that those readers who have a mind to enhance a listening or other skill can do so in a framework which will maximise the chance of success.

In the next chapter, we look at questioning and assertiveness.

6

◆ Questioning and Assertiveness ◆

INTRODUCTION

We look first at questioning, a key skill which the assertive persuader has in his armoury. Then we draw together and develop our thinking on assertive attitudes and behaviour, at the heart of effective persuasion in the one-to-one situation.

QUESTIONING

One of the most commonly used forms of questioning is closed questioning (see Figure 38).

As the figure indicates, such questioning closes down conversation and limits exploration as it demands only yes or no answers.

Let us take an example. An individual is given the following facts and asked to uncover the truth – but only by deploying closed questions.

The facts are:

- A man is pushing a car
- The car stops next to a hotel
- The man realises he is bankrupt

The questioning proceeded in one case as follows:

Q: Does he own the hotel?

A: No.

Q: Has the car run out of petrol?

A: No.

Q: Does he own the car?

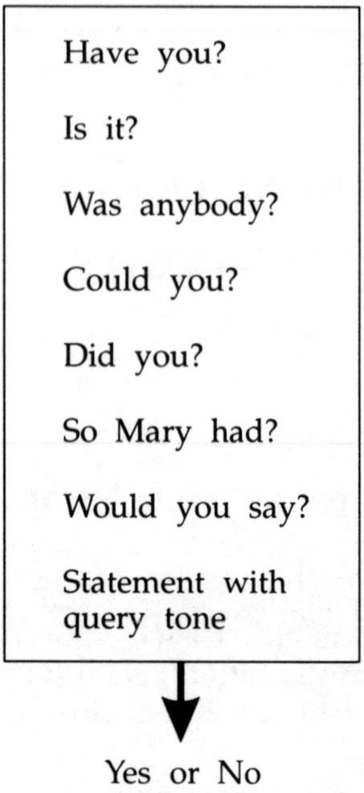

Have you?

Is it?

Was anybody?

Could you?

Did you?

So Mary had?

Would you say?

Statement with query tone

Yes or No

Figure 38 Closed questions

A: Yes.

Q: Is he running some sort of business; or is he a driver; or is he running a car firm?

A: No.

Q: Does he rely on his business from the hotel?

A: No.

Q: Is it a person at the hotel that gives him information?

A: No.

Q: Is the hotel in financial trouble?

A: No.

(Pause)
[The car's broken down and he's pushing it.
(Pause) Maybe the car hasn't broken down]

Q: Has the car broken down?

A: No.

Q: Has he lost the ignition key?

A: No.

Q: Is there a shortage of oil or some sort of petrol crisis?

A: No.

Q: Has the car got a puncture?

A: No.

Q: Has he locked himself out of the car?

A: No.

(Increasing tones of frustration and annoyance) [So why is he pushing it? He owns it and it's not broken down] (Pause)

Q: Is it the condition of the road that stops him driving it?

A: No.

Q: Does he want it to stop at the hotel?

A: No.

[Bloody hell. Why would it stop at the hotel, if he doesn't want it to?]

Q: Has a policeman stopped the car?

A: No.

(Pause)

Q: Does the man read something to tell him he is bankrupt?

A: No.

[OK! This is stupid. I give up]

The answer was that the man was playing Monopoly (using the car and not the boot, hat, ship etc), landed on a site with a hotel and realised the rental demand exceeded all his assets, even when mortgaged!

Closed questions are the ally of the ego persuader, or those using Incentives or Logic. They are used far too frequently by all of us, and are a major barrier to effective communication and assertive persuasion.

They have their place in the scheme of things, as we will see. But if we are going to uncover others' knowledge, feelings and attitudes, if we are going to become more creative, we have to deploy *open questions*.

> 'I keep six honest serving men,
> They taught me all I know,
> Their names are What and Why and When
> and How and Where and Who'

Rudyard Kipling

How simple it would have been, if the rules of the question game above had permitted the question: 'What is the explanation of the situation?'

Instead false assumptions were made, thoughts were locked into unfruitful lines of questioning, the questioning itself at times was unhelpful, frustration and disbelief set in, and anger and annoyance at the respondent peeped out. Have we ever been in that situation, and blamed others not ourselves?

In the persuasion situation, we should deploy a judicious mix of questions, using closed questions to establish the facts, open questions to establish the knowledge and emotional base, and closed questions to bring matters to a conclusion.

Take an identical scenario, one handled by an ego persuader, and the other by an assertive persuader.

EP: Chris tells me that you were late again this morning. Is that correct?

A: Yes, I'm very sorry.

EP: In fact, you were more than half-an-hour late. Am I right?

A: Yes. (mumbled)

EP: To be completely accurate (and you know I like to have my facts right), you have been more than half-an-hour late every day this week, have you not?

A: Yes.

EP: Well, this firm(!) does not tolerate laziness and unpunctuality. I am a fair man (as you know), but I don't beat about the bush. If this occurs once more, we(!) will start the disciplinary procedure against you. Do I make myself clear?

A: Yes

EP: Well don't let it happen again.

If we were to ask EP what the problem was, he would say that it was his 'subordinate' (or, in fact, his subordinate's subordinate) being late for work. If we asked EP what his objective was, he would say that it was to ensure the 'subordinate' stopped being late. If we were to ask EP, at the end of this encounter, whether he had succeeded, he would say 'yes'.

Notice the language that shows the dominance of Logic and Incentives. Notice the closed questions, enabling EP to follow his logic, without regard to the subordinate's position. Notice the use of the word 'firm', like some fathers use the word 'family'. The use tries to conjure another authority beyond the self. It fact it is just an alternate ego, quite well concealed from the gullible or brainwashed.

Notice also the subtle 'we', enabling his junior manager to carry out the formal disciplinary procedure and not EP.

Now EP might believe his own story, but we know differently, do we not? (Rhetorical closed question!) His primary objective was to flaunt his power and abuse another person. He certainly succeeded.

Let us turn to the approach of our friend assertive persuader – AP. Now AP likes to solve problems and concentrate on behaviour, not the person. He also recognises that there is a difference between a symptom and a cause!

AP: Chris tells me that you were over half-an-hour late this morning, and, in fact, every morning this week. Is that correct?

A: Yes. I'm very sorry.

AP: Tell me why were you late.

A: Well, the traffic's been very bad.

AP: But the traffic's always bad, and you normally come to work on time. So, what's the problem?

A: Well ... My mother's very poorly.

AP: I'm sorry to hear that, John. It must be very tough for you, as you are very close to your mother.

A: Yes, Alex, it's tough alright.

AP: (Pause) But, I don't see why you are late, John.

A: Well, mother now needs our full-time care. She can't be left on her own for a minute. Barbara, my wife, works

nights and doesn't get back home until half-past eight. I
immediately set off for work, but because of the traffic,
I'm late.

AP: I see. And because you want to get home as soon
as possible to relieve Barbara, who must be tired out,
you have left work at the normal time, rather than
making the time up?

A: Yes and no, Alex. I have left at the normal time, but
I have cut my lunch hour down to half-an-hour, and
made the time up that way.

AP: I've no problem with that at all. This whole
position must be causing you and Barbara a lot of
stress. Are there any alternatives we can think of that
will help matters, I wonder. Have you tried to get
help from 'Home Help' for instance.

A: No we haven't actually. This has all happened very
suddenly – last week-end in fact.

AP: Well, why don't you take the rest of the day off,
and see if you can set the wheels in motion. Then we
can have a chat tomorrow on progress. We have to
get the short-term fixed quickly, but there is also the
longer term to consider.

A: Thanks ever so much, Alec.

A different approach, a different outcome! Notice the closed
question to establish the facts, not to prolong the agony as EP did
by separating them out. Then there was the open 'why' question,
with any abruptness taken out with the preface 'tell me'. (Variations are: 'So tell me why'; 'Will you please tell me why'; 'I would
appreciate it if you would tell me why' and so on).

The excuse is countered with rational logic, followed by a direct
open question. The verbal (and it can be assumed tone and body
language) reflection of the persuadee's feeling followed, and then
the short empathetic pause. But AP is not distracted, and continues
the logical approach with another 'why'. Then he makes an
assumption, but in a supportive and not controlling way. Because
of the mood or ambience created, John has the confidence to
remove that assumption. A supportive closed question begins to
wind matters down, and an action plan is agreed.

This short cameo indicates the key aspects of assertive persuasion – a combination of rational logic and empathy, developed

through a judicious mix of closed and open questions and effective listening.

Before considering the type of questions an assertive persuader would avoid and why, I would mention one important use of closed questions – to support social rituals.

Have you ever come back to work on a Monday morning, encountered a colleague, and had a conversation along the lines of:

'Hi, Charles, did you have a nice weekend?'
'Yes thanks. and you, Paul?'
'Not bad, at all. A bit parky this morning. Still spring's just round the corner, so we musn't grumble.'
'Too true. See you.'
'Bye.'

Thank God for closed questions! And how do we feel, if the ritual is disturbed by a colleague who has had a bad weekend, and actually wants to talk about it?

QUESTIONS TO AVOID

There are a number of questions that an assertive persuader should avoid, as they reduce the probability of positive outcomes.

Long complicated questions

On a video, we have a persuasion role-play between two managers, where one took more than ten minutes to ask his question. You should have seen the body language of the listener! If we are not confident, or we are too involved, or we are too rushed and are speaking before we think(!), we can get lost. We can start a question, go on a gentle ramble or lecture tour, recover, and revert back to the question in hand.

This is to be avoided, as it makes us look silly, and puts the listener to sleep! We should keep our questions simple and to the point.

'Or' questions

'Or' questions should be avoided for two reasons. If 'or' is used conjunctively ie both alternatives can be selected, the question is self-defeating.

Q: Did you go to the cinema or the theatre?

A: Yes.

There was an amusing example of this recently, when a back-bench Labour MP put forward written questions, intended to embarrass the government by showing the extent of sex discrimination in the Civil Service. Unfortunately, he ended by asking whether men or women were employed! The junior minister's written reply to the entire set of questions was one word – yes.

If 'or' is used disjunctively ie one of the alternatives must be selected, the question acts as a constraint by forcing choice between the two alternatives. This limits creativity ie the exploration of other options. Such an approach would be valid when exploration of all the options uncovered has led to only two being practical or possible *and* they are mutually exclusive.

However, a cultural consequence of an excess of logical thinking is that we tend to close down before we have opened up.

Multiple questions

A golden rule of effective questioning is 'one at a time'. More than one question can lead to confusion as to which the persuadee should answer or it can lead to evasion. The persuadee can select which one to answer, and the other one or ones can be lost in the subsequent discussion.

This is what happened to the unfortunate MP.

Leading questions

'Surely you do not have any doubts about our new mission?' We are leading the persuadee to the required response, which accords with our views, not made explicit.

Loaded questions

'Do you not agree that John has poor time-keeping?' This is very similar to a leading question. The difference is that our opinions are explicitly loaded into the question.

Staccato style

While it is right to follow the rule 'one at a time', we should avoid a battering ram approach. If we do adopt such a style, then we know that we are using too many closed questions. You cannot batter with open ones. It is perceived, whether intended or not, as interrogation.

We should not be menu-driven when we persuade. Have you ever experienced a situation when the persuader or interviewer went through a predetermined checklist of questions, mentally or physically ticking off the answers, without ever listening? Most discomforting from the other side of the table, and rather unproductive.

Focus and structure

A point we will develop in Chapter 9 is the need to provide a focus and structure for the questions so that they are related, in the right order and in the right context.

ASSERTIVENESS

The value and importance of an assertive approach to persuasion has been a major theme. We have considered assertiveness to some extent already, and shown how effective listening and questioning are key skills in being effectively assertive.

In this final section, I develop some of the key themes.

There can be a cultural bias in the teaching and understanding of assertiveness. There is a tendency to adopt an ego approach. In other words the assertive individual asserts her rights. She is not submissive, allowing her rights to be trampled on, nor aggressive, trampling on others' rights. However the focus is on the individual exercising her rights in a non-aggressive way.

If we remove that bias, we introduce the principle of mutuality. Yes, indeed, when we are assertive, we stick up for our rights. But we do more. We assert others' rights. We recognise and stick up for their rights. We empower ourselves, and we empower others. We try to make the submissive assertive. If we fail, we will lapse into aggression. We try to make the aggressive assertive. If we fail, we will lapse into aggression or submission.

That is the approach of the assertive persuader. It is based on self-respect, otherwise we will be aggressive or submissive. Aggressive if we use conscious overconfidence and desire to control to create certainty and still that inner voice of doubt and darkness. Submissive if we look to others to provide what we cannot find in ourselves.

It is based on respect for others, without which we can only be aggressive.

Assertiveness is first and foremost a state of mind – a belief. However, to be effective we need to develop skill through practising techniques like effective questioning and listening.

I finish with the assertive code – recognising that some

organisational cultures make it more difficult to be assertive than others!

THE ASSERTIVE CODE

- To respect myself and others.
- To make mistakes, to admit them and to learn from them. To allow others to make mistakes and help them learn from them.
- To express my views and opinions and encourage others to do the same.
- To listen and be listened to.
- To say how I feel as well as think, and encourage others to do likewise.
- As a leader, to explicitly agree with my followers their job responsibilities, objectives, and performance standards. To help them achieve their objectives, and to provide regular feedback on their performance. To discipline the follower, when he has been provided with support and failed to meet the agreed standards.
- As a follower, to ensure that I know and accept my responsibilities, objectives and performance standards, to work to the best of my ability, to know how my leader sees my performance, and to refuse unreasonable requests that are not part of my responsibilities.

7

◆ Creativity ◆

In this and the next chapter, we look at skills and techniques to improve our capability to persuade groups of people rather than just individuals. Our role-model is the VTL. The profile is set out below.

The VTL can be thought of as an individual who has achieved the final stage of development and competence. Assertive persuasion is the significant milestone on the way. In the one-to-one context, the VTL operates as an assertive persuader, with the added dimensions of a well-developed creative ability, and focus on group motivators such as corporate vision and mission and

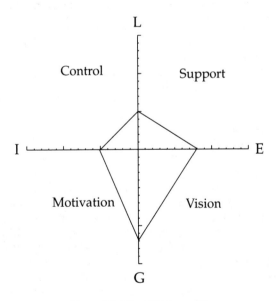

Figure 39 The VTL's profile

departmental or team goals, as well as individual motivators. This increases the probability and quality of win/win outcomes.

The key differentiators or development areas from the assertive persuader are: the focus on the group as well as the individual; *and* the ability to catalyse group synergy – to create an environment of shared understanding and commitment to a common vision and agreed goals, and the skill to empower the team-members to achieve those goals.

So we look at creativity in this chapter. In the next, we examine something called facilitation (at the heart of empowerment), focusing on what works and why.

CREATIVITY

We can all be more creative than we are. It's just that most of us have been taught how to think logically and not creatively. As a result, most of us are uncomfortable with ideas and creative people – fear of the unknown and the different. Individually and organisationally, we can put the mockers on creativity, using our highly developed logical skills to support nurtured prejudice.

This is unfortunate in a world of change, where the development and application of ideas is vital to long-term survival. Ideas solve problems, improve situations, generate opportunities and innovations, are the lubricant to invention, and are at the heart of vision.

Ideas are a jolly good idea!

Change means doing things differently. To do things differently means thinking creatively. Much more is required. Vision provides the group motivation and sense of direction. Vision is necessarily long-term ie a number of years out – a horizon, not a step in a logical progression. Vision paints the picture of the different world we want to create, whether at a national, corporate, team or individual level. The mission is a concrete statement of the vision. Key action areas and long-term objectives in those areas tell us where we have to focus our activities and how we know whether we have succeeded or failed and the extent of either. Interim milestones towards long-term objectives define the route map and progress. Finally, actions prioritised over time set us on the path to success – doing things differently but strategically directed towards achieving our mission and realising our vision.

I will return to this process in the final chapter Planning to Improve. I mention it now to emphasise that effective change takes time, and is an evolutionary process to achieve a revolutionary goal. Secondly, there is no dichotomy between logic and creativity. Ideas on their own produce wasted thought. Logic on its own produces wasted action.

It is the application of each skill in the right context and the right order that produces effective action.

There are a number of simple approaches and techniques, which will enhance our creative contribution to effective action.

Time

If we spend five minutes trying to think creatively, taking that pause from the heat of logic and action, we will have fewer ideas than if we spend half-an-hour. So we need to invest our time. Clearly the law of diminishing returns sets in – eventually the more time we spend the less ideas we have, and the more frustrated we become. If we eat a watermelon, we eat one slice at a time, and we don't (usually!) gobble it all up in one go. The same with creative thinking. But we take a nice, juicy bite rather than a quick nibble.

Belief

Unless we believe in the importance and value of creativity, we won't ever be any good. If we don't want to do something, we won't do it very well. There are exceptions. Fear, pain and the like can push us on. This is not a very constructive approach though. If we are thrust back to the animal, we cannot develop the human.

Suspending judgement

If you turn back to the second chapter, you will see that I mentioned that logic is the enemy of creativity. The logical and creative thinking process are separate. We are creative when generating ideas and logical when evaluating them. If we evaluate before we create or as we create, we build nothing. We are left with the building we have already constructed - the very edifice that either needs knocking down or a major extension.

Edward de Bono in one of his seminars explained this to me very well.

Let us turn to Figure 40.

The brain operates in a very large, but finite number of stable states. The points A and C are in one such state, and B is in another. Each state comprises a routine thought pattern, and represents a wide catchment area for the external stimuli the brain receives. So something provokes our thinking, which starts, say, in the first stable state. The brain likes to remain where it is happy. Other things being equal, we think inside the pattern of thought in our stable state. We start at A, say, and move in a logical, linear, routine and comfortable way to C. C is not the place to be (!), because it represents 'the one right answer', with which we are logically satisfied, or no answer at all (there will be examples in a minute), which can be a very frustrating.

Where we want to be, although we don't know it, when locked into the AC pattern of thought, is B. This is because B is a very good solution to our problem. How do we get to B, if the brain is naturally disinclined to move out of its comfort zone?

We give it a good kick up the B-side! We provoke it. We deliberately abandon logic by a non-logical provocation. This jerks our brains outside the comfort zone. This is an excellent start, but we have a problem. We are uncomfortable sitting in a discomfort zone with no logic nor structure. We are keen to move back into a stable state, and enjoy some more of those lovely routine thought patterns as soon as possible. Two things can happen. As we are closest to the AC pattern, we bring in our little logical friend – judgement – apply it to this illogical provocation and, hey presto, we are back in the AC state, shivering slightly at our nasty experience, soon forgotten. Alternatively, we suspend judgement, 'go with the flow' and move further and further away from AC. Then, all of a sudden, we are sitting in the B state.

CREATIVITY

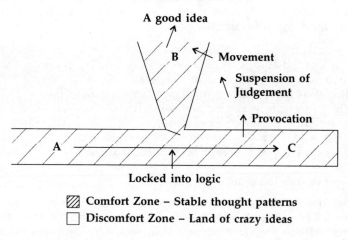

Figure 40 The path to creativity

The key feature of B is that it is another stable state, with a nice routine thought pattern. In fact, after the event, we recognise logically how we moved from A to B. We connect B to A, so that the B state is now an extension of the AC state. We only recognise an idea as sound if we can make these logical connections after this non-logical process. If we don't make the connection, we won't accept the idea. In other words, ideas cannot be generated by logical foresight, but are always logically recognised in hindsight.

It is a paradox that the more logical we are, the less creative we are *and* the more creative we could be. If we overcome the resistance to creativity generated by our powerful logical minds by applying such provocations or other techniques, we will come up with more ideas than those who are less logically developed (but perceived as more creative) than us.

This reality has been amply demonstrated to me. I have trained many lawyers with highly developed logical and analytical skills. Additionally, I have trained many managers and executives. The lawyers have been far, far more resistant to creative thinking. One, who was particularly dominant and negative, particularly well-developed logically, and with an extremely closed mind, destroyed a creative thinking session for himself, his colleagues and me. He denied not only the value of creativity but the fact that creative thinking existed. He argued that all ideas were logically generated. There was only logical thinking. He had a powerful case, as all ideas can be connected back to the starting point *after* the non-logical creative act. So any idea he had had (and he had had some excellent ones) could be generated now by logical foresight. They were not new ideas, but part of routine thought patterns. They had expanded the knowledge base.

Equally, on those occasions when their minds were sufficiently open to understand, accept and apply creative thinking techniques, the quality and range of their ideas were outstanding.

I will illustrate further deliberate provocations in the section after next, but first I want to cover humour.

Humour

Humour (not sarcasm nor biting wit) is our best creative friend. When we laugh together, we are being creative as well as having fun. The process involved in humour parallels that of deliberate provocation.

We will not laugh if we understand the punchline in advance, we cannot work out the punchline (provided we have not heard the joke before and we dig into memory) by logical thinking from our existing pattern, and we only laugh if we can make logical connections backwards, when we have heard the punchline.

If we can't make the connections, we don't laugh. How often do others around us laugh, and we are not amused? Assuming we ask for an explanation, then we will only appreciate the joke and chuckle if we understand it – logically! We will chuckle rather than laugh as the mood has gone, and we were not part of the group infection that enhances the power of the joke and increases the volume and intensity of the laughter. I am sure we can all recall when the group becomes downright silly – a prolonged, near-hysterical event occurs, where comments, repetitions and new slants provoke more and more laughter and emotion. In the cold light of logical day, they appear stupid. It is the same with effective group brainstorming. Creativity is enhanced by the mood and the humour and the abandonment of logic.

Let us take one of a million examples.

Mother: Come on, John, eat your breakfast; you'll be
            late for school.

John: I don't want to go to school. The teachers don't like
            me, the children don't like me – even the caretaker
            doesn't like me!

Mother: All the same, you must go.

John: Why should I?

Before the punchline, which I will conceal in the subsequent text, I would ask you to put your thinking hat on and come up with what you think Mother's reply was.

Provocation

Deliberate

As we have seen, one way of being more creative is to identify a key feature or features of the problem you want to solve or situation you want to improve, and deliberately reverse or exaggerate it. This is a technique invented by Edward de Bono.

We already had the example of this in Chapter 2, where the insurance executive was considering what new insurance product they could introduce in the life insurance market to generate more sales and profits. A key feature was that the proceeds were paid after death. The provocation was a reversal 'you die before you die' and the successful product was a new policy, which paid out three-quarters of the death benefit to policy holders who were terminally ill, before they died.

This was a breakthrough in thinking which became an industry standard product. Clearly, you cannot die before you die, and the use of logic would have destroyed the ability to create the new product. It seems very logical afterwards.

'Well, clearly, if we know precisely when they are going to die, we can afford to pay out some of the proceeds before they actually do, perhaps charging a little early payment fee! The beneficiaries will be delighted to get their hands on the money sooner rather than later. The policy holder probably couldn't care less, or will be relieved that the costs of care will be covered or will like to see his beloved ones enjoying the money before he passes on – depending on the circumstances. A very logically sound proposition, which will improve our image and our profits. I am really rather surprised I didn't think up the idea myself!'

Another example was the US in the 1970s, suffering an increase in crime. Some deliberately provocative thinking was carried out by decision-takers. They focused on policemen, and examined some key features – literally. One feature, to which they applied a deliberate exaggeration, was policemen's eyes. Normally, policemen, like the rest of us, have two. 'Policemen have six eyes' lead to the introduction of Neighbourhood Watch, subsequently transported to the UK.

So there is a lot of power in deliberate, structured provocation. Try it.

However, there are many other sources of provocation, which will make us more creative.

Dreams

Some people write down their dreams. It is a good idea. We are marvellously constructed. If we won't solve our problems consciously, locked into logic, action, assumption and continuity, then our subconscious tries to help us out. It creates a dream world of discontinuity and no logic, the ideal breeding ground for the crazy and not so crazy ideas. We should listen to the message of our dreams. To do so, we need to write them down, as the vision dies so quickly.

'Let's sleep on it' is very sound advice.

I remember that, every week for nearly ten years, I dreamt I was back at school or university, studying for examinations, or re-sitting actual exams or failing exams or passing exams brilliantly or similar themes presented in different ways with different slants.

I knew I was deeply unhappy with the quality of my degree, but I did not listen. Eventually I did and got another, better one. The dreams ceased.

Day-dreaming or wishful thinking plays a similar role. 'Wouldn't be nice if', 'If only', 'I wonder what would happen if'.

Mood

We have already mentioned the power of humour as a creative tool. Equally, relaxing, letting go, doing regular solo activity of a non-stressful physical nature creates a mood or environment when we can just stop thinking in a logical way. We let our minds go, and off they wander. We feel better for it, and sometimes we have good ideas.

Questioning assumptions

'Why' is the most powerful of Kipling's 'six serving men', followed by 'How'. We have already seen how important why is. Questioning our own and others' assumptions in an assertive way is critical for effective persuasion, and improves our creative skills. We should question assumptions deliberately and consciously.

It is being locked into unquestioned, and invalid assumption, supported by logic that denies us creativity.

Let us return to John and his mother. The mother's final reply, providing the punchline was: 'Because you are 45 and the headmaster!' We may have assumed that John was a child, may we not?

How do you plant four identical cylindrical stakes, so that each stake is exactly the same distance from every other stake? Distance is measured from the centre of the cylinder.

So have a go, assuming you have not come across this particular problem before. Please don't forage out the answer until you have an answer or have given up. You might also like to put your mental tentacles around the following people – situation problems.

- A man drives his child to school. On the way, the car is involved in an accident and the child is seriously injured. The child is rushed to hospital, and into the operating theatre. The surgeon takes a look at the child and says: 'Oh, my God, it's my son.' Explain.
- A woman jumps from the top of a New York skyscraper. It is a deliberate act of suicide. As she tumbles to her death, she hears a telephone ring. She cries out: 'I wish I had not jumped.' Explain her behaviour.

■ A man falls asleep. He wakes up a few hours later, turns on the radio, and hears that, while he slept, there has been a terrible disaster. He looks up and sees the light is out. He commits suicide. Why?

Sorry about the morbid theme!

There is one more problem I would like you to consider. It is not the same as the other three, but I introduce it here so that the answer will be well-hidden in the text, and can be considered at the right moment. The problem can be solved by a flash of inspiration, a good memory if you have heard it before, or by a combination of focus, visualisation and provocation.

A man is in the middle of an island surrounded by deep water. He is looking after a flock of sheep. (Don't worry how he and the sheep got there. You can assume an omnipotent intervention or you are in a dream). The island is covered by very tall grass, which is bone dry. A fire has started (omnipotent causation!) at the end of the island, furthest away from the sheep and the man. There is a wall of flame moving very slowly towards the man and his sheep. The wind is blowing directly towards the man, and will remain in the same direction throughout.

How do the man and all the sheep remain alive and unburnt, given that, if they enter the water, they will all drown?

Before looking at the answers, I would mention that the four-stake problem has produced some interesting reactions. The tutor who set it for my group when I attended a general management development programme some years ago mentioned that a colleague (an 'I am cleverer than you' character) had actually been hit by a delegate. The individual was incensed at what he saw as a waste of time, a trick question with no answer and a know-all tutor to boot. The unwise tutor had let them stew for a quarter of an hour!

I never let contemplation of this question last more than a few minutes! Even so, I occasionally receive dark mutterings: 'Trick question. There is no answer.'

I didn't answer it, and the majority do not. Let us explore possibilities. Putting the stakes in a square doesn't work, as each pole is the same distance from two others, but not the one on the diagonal opposite. Putting them on the circumference of a circle or with three on the circumference and one at the centre will lead to a variety of configurations, all of which are inferior to the perfect square, which is one such configuration. Putting them together produces a square of dots! Putting them in a line means each has at least one other stake further from it than another. Putting them on top of each other, burying three in the ground is similar to putting them in a line. However, the last thought, if it occurs to us, may lead to the breakthrough.

The answer is to plant three stakes in the same plane in the shape of an equilateral triangle and the fourth on the top of a hillock or the bottom of a hollow, so as to form a tetrahedron or triangular pyramid. The face of each side is in the form of an equilateral triangle – as shown in Figure 41.

The problem cannot be solved if we stay in two dimensions – make an invalid assumption that we fail to question! As most such assumptions are implicit and unquestioned, we have to stand back – get into the helicopter – and identify the assumptions we are making. Then we examine those to see how many are immutable – are an integral part of the necessary structure - and how many can be changed. When we play with those that can be changed, eradicating or altering, we have a new insight, a new perspective, and find the answer or a better way.

Turning now to the other three questions, there is the answer for the first and answers for the next two. The beauty of creativity is that it does not necessarily lead to 'the one right answer'. The power of creativity is that it can lead to a whole host of answers or alternatives. Many of those alternatives, which are not mutually exclusive, can all be implemented over time. That is how situations can be radically altered for the better – the vision realised.

- The surgeon is the boy's mother. Many assume that the surgeon is male. I wonder why?
- The key to a range of answers is whether you spot the use of the indefinite article! The question states 'a' telephone, not 'the' telephone. The implication is that the caller is not known by the woman. Many people assume 'the' and create stories around the caller having some form of relationship with the women. That's no bad thing, as ideas are good for their own sake – improving our creative powers.

  There are a number of stories that come from a recognition of the 'a'. One is that there has been a neutron holocaust, killing nearly all the people in the world, but leaving the infrastructure unaffected. The poor woman has spent hours and days and months trying to contact a fellow human being – to no avail. At last, unable to bear the threat of total isolation, she jumps. As she tumbles to her death, she hears that ring. She is not alone, and cries out before she dies: 'I wish I had not jumped.'

- There are two possible assumptions. The man's job is a conventional job, and the light is a conventional light. Again I have heard a number of stories. One is that the radio

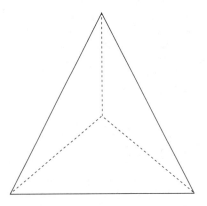

Figure 41 A tetrahedron

spokesperson has announced that there has been a shipwreck, causing substantial loss of life. The man is the lighthouse keeper, who allowed the light to go out, because he slept. He was responsible for the tragedy. He could not bear the pain and guilt, and so took his own life.

Visualisation

A picture's worth a thousand words. While dreaming or daydreaming is unfocused or unstructured visualisation, here I am talking about deliberate visualisation.

Visualisation is an excellent way of improving memory, as well as creativity. A couple of examples. Say that you have an appointment with the dentist the next day before you go to work. As you go to sleep, you imagine putting a very large (exaggeration again!) tube of toothpaste into the right shoe, left beside your bed. Dwell on the image – then sleep soundly. As you put your foot in your right shoe, you will remember, if you have not already. Try it – it works. After all, pieces of paper can get lost.

You have a vital business presentation to make. Imagine the whole process – collecting your bits and bobs together, travelling to the client and making the presentation. It's amazing what you will remember, which you might have overlooked or overlook – like phoning up the client to ensure there is an overhead projector for your snazzy visuals!

Visualisation is also a powerful generator of ideas. Let us return to the man and his sheep and combine focus, visualisation and provocation.

Pareto, a seventeenth century Italian philosopher, created the 80/20 rule. For instance, 20 per cent of clients produce 80 per cent of profits or 20 per cent of shareholders own 80 per cent of the company or 20 per cent of our time produces 80 per cent of results! Recognising this approximate truth enables focus. Similarly, we are bombarded with an excess of information, where 20 per cent (or often much less) provides 80 per cent (or often nearly all) the meaning. So we should focus on extracting the key messages and concentrate on those.

Take our man-and-sheep problem and see what key messages we can uncover. A good starting point is the open question: 'What is available to the man to save his own and the sheep's lives?' It should be clear that the water is a no go area. That leaves the sheep, the man with his strength and intelligence, the wind, the grass and the fire.

Sheep are large, awkward and stupid creatures. Avenues of thought like the man picking up a sheep and trying to put the fire out with it lead only to cul-de-sacs. Any such sheep so deployed would be somewhat severely burnt. So with our focus hat on, let us assume that the sheep are passive bystanders, and turn to the wind.

Now the fact that the wind is moving in the same direction must have significance or it would not have been mentioned. This looks like a hindrance, but perhaps it is a help or clue to the answer?

Let us get into our helicopters and visualise events over time. This should help our thinking. If we hover at a safe distance, we initially see a thin orange line, a little bit of black behind it, a substantial amount of green, slowly being eaten by the orange and the dots of the man and his sheep. As time passes, the black area expands and the green contracts. Eventually the yellow line disappears and the dots no longer move – all is black. In our contemplative mood, we may notice that black is the sign of death – yet it is also a safety zone. If the man and his sheep were magically transported to a black zone, they would safe. Fortunately the man is a magician, as we will see.

Now, let us indulge deliberately in a bit of illogical thinking ourselves, while still in that helicopter. A, if not the, key feature is the constant wind direction, bringing death in its wake. Let us reverse it! What do we see? We see the line of fire falter, change direction briefly, before dying down and out. We see a black area and a green area, with the man and his sheep safe.

The reversal and related concepts run deep in creativity. Let us magically and safely alight, and become the man – reverse our viewpoint. From the man's perspective, under this magic scenario, he sees a wall of fire moving away from him briefly. Now the man cannot reverse the direction of the wind, but can he create a situation where he sees fire moving away from him? If he does, he and his sheep will be safe.

Now, the wind is moving very slowly. What messages does that contain? The man has plenty of time to implement any stratagem is one, and another is that the man can outrun the wind.

What about the fire? Shall we play with fire, have some fire fantasies, imagine the old Greek Gods hurling thunderbolts at each other – fighting fire with fire? The concept may simply flash into minds because of the consequence of creative thinking and visualisation. I have often thought that the mind, when in a creative mode, is both free and intensely active, operating at the highest level. What often occurs for me and others, when in that thinking mode, is a spark. It's as if the top of our brains have come into electrifying contact with some external stimuli, waiting to give. All of a sudden, that new idea, that flash of inspiration, that was not, is. We can try to be too scientific or even logical about creativity! Whether or not we think of fighting fire with fire, we still have to consider the grass. How can the man use the grass to save himself? Have you got the answer, assuming you failed on your own?

As is often the case, the answer is simple. The man produces a fire-break. He grabs some grass, twists it together, runs to the fire and lights the grass rope. He runs away from the fire, past the sheep to the other end of the island and starts his own little fire. Fire fighting fire and one fire moving away from him! The wind proceeds at its majestic pace. The initial fire bears slowly down, and the new fire creeps to the end of the island, where it splutters and expires, leaving that now comforting and safe black zone. The man waits to the last moment, and herds his sheep to safety.

Techniques

There are other specific techniques that can be used to generate ideas, whether on one's own or in a group. This book is not a creative thinking book *per se*, and I would refer you to writers like Edward de Bono or Tony Buzanne (mind mapping). However, I will share with you a very pragmatic process I have developed, based on Kiplings 'six serving men'. We will consider a very relevant issue to this book and the VTL – 'increasing the use of creative thinking in an organisation'.

Why?

Until and if we think that an issue is worth addressing (whether a problem to be solved, a situation to be improved, an opportunity to be seized or vision to be created), there is no point addressing it. The first realty is that, at the minimum, we must own the issue.

I hope that the case for improving individual and organisational creativity has been made. It is an assumption I am explicitly making.

How?

Let's go for it. Let us have some ideas – and we can be ridiculous and illogical, use reversal, visualisation and provocation, once we are in the mood. We should try to avoid being downright silly, which can occur in group creativity sessions, covered in the final section.

Here are a few. We are reacting to the specific trigger of 'How can we make our organisation more creative?':

1. Sack the managing director.

2. Ban ideas (reversal).

3. Eradicate logic.

4. Find time.

5. Introduce suggestion boxes.

6. Send the top decision takers on a creative thinking programme.

7. Give prizes.

8. Build a crazy-idea room.

9. Wear funny hats.

10. Start a joke competition.

11. Change the reward system.

12. Change the culture.

13. Set targets.

14. Deploy techniques.

15. Train managers and staff.

16. Hire experts.

17. Generate success stories.

18. Solve real problems.

19. Spread the gospel.

20. Ask the customer.

21. Find champions.

22. Go off-site.

It's only a few minutes' work, and the range of ideas will increase in a group context, because of the sparks that will fly one to the other and out of the ether.

Fine, we have twenty-two ideas. What do we do next? Sometimes, I hate these open questions!

What?

That's what we do. We ask the 'what' question. So what is the theme behind each idea or suggestion? Why do we ask this what question? To build in structure, which will assist in further creativity and provide focus. We identify the key themes. Let us do so, in reverse order.

What is the theme behind 'going off-site', suggestion number 22. It is to produce a positive environment. Improving the environment is one theme, the themes behind 8 and 9. The theme behind 21, find champions is generating ownership, the theme behind 17,18, and 19.

The theme behind 20, ask the customer, is establishing the need. The theme behind 16, hire experts, is to develop expertise, the themes behind 15 and 14 and 6.

The theme behind 13, set targets, is to increase motivation, the theme behind 5,7,10 and 11. Change the culture, 12 is a theme in itself, as is 4, find time. The theme behind 1 and 3 is reduce resistance. The final suggestion 2, ban ideas is a wild one, which goes into its own box. Incidentally, it could have generated (and did) a number of ideas, and is worth retaining for development.

(For instance, if you had no ideas at all, corporate life would grind to a halt. Perhaps the managing director or some other key decision takers are action, logical men, dismissive of 'woolly thinking' or creativity. They are significant barriers to increasing creativity in the company. We could demonstrate to them that the use of logic alone leads to absurdities. We could show how papers they had written, which they thought contained pure logic, contained quite a few excellent ideas. Perhaps we could build up a picture in their minds that logic on its own was a disaster, ideas are very important, they were very creative, and perhaps they should enhance their considerable talents by attending an exclusive two day seminar on creativity!)

Now there is a terrible tendency for 'experts' to wave magic wands and say this is so and 'Are you not impressed?' We are left struggling trying to work out how the hell they got to the answer. Creative gurus are no exception. I am not a creative guru.

We take ideas, identify themes, and the ideas which are not themes are *action areas*. Each suggestion is one or the other. Identifying which is which is a piece of cake! Take 'find time'. That is amenable to the 'how' question ie how to find time or increase time. 'Increasing time for creativity' is a *theme*. Take 'set targets'. How to set targets is a small process issue, already known. What targets should be set identifies targets as an *action area*. If it is an action area, it is not a theme. We still have to identify the theme. What theme lies behind setting targets or why should we set targets? Answer, to increase motivation. That is the theme.

The process is set out schematically in Figures 42 and 43.

Once you have established a subset of themes, you go to each one, and are creative again eg, 'How to increase time spent on creative thinking' and so on. You will end up with a number of action areas. There will be a measure of duplication as the themes may overlap (reducing resistance and generating ownership), or the same action area comes from different themes. This doesn't matter one iota. The whole point of creativity is to open up and explore the possible, avoiding the one right answer or no answer at all. In fact, provided you don't have silly brainstorms and keep the wild ideas to deliberate provocations, you will end up with all the material for a powerful and effective strategic action plan – without having to spend an inordinate amount of time!

The final phase is to take each action area and use 'what' again. What targets could be set. This leads to a list of alternative actions.

With this process complete, you can move into the evaluation and planning phase – deciding what the time frame for implementation should be, what the long-term objectives are, what alternatives are practical and not mutually exclusive, what the resource implications are, what are the priorities in which area, and the sequence of the actions.

GROUP CREATIVITY

Becoming more creative assists the assertive persuader in his one-to-one interactions and the VTL in his group interactions.

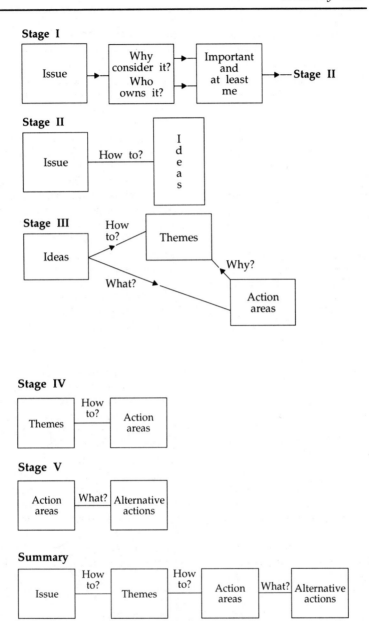

Figure 42 A creative thinking process

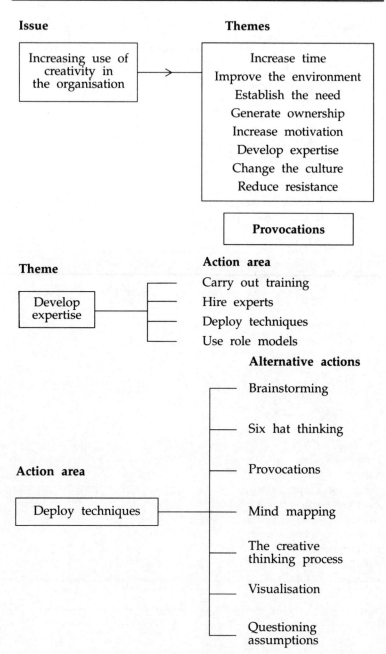

Figure 43 An example of thinking creatively

However, the VTL also needs to manage group creativity or 'brainstorming' to enhance the creative contribution of the team as a whole and develop team spirit and focus.

After all, at the heart of visioning is creativity. For the VTL, this is a shared group process.

There is one golden rule of effective brain-storming: *There should be no criticism by word, tone of voice or body language of any idea expressed.*

I am sure that you appreciate the reason behind the rule – judgement is the enemy of creativity. Have you been at a meeting, when you have been a team-member and not leader, and the purpose has been to solve a problem? Have you found that the voice that is heard to the exclusion of others, including your own, was the chairman? Has there been, as a result, the one right answer – his?

If anyone criticises, it stops the flow from the individual criticised (and, let's face it, criticising the idea is also criticising the individual), inhibits others not yet criticised, denies the chance of building a creative atmosphere, which is vital, and hence destroys any chance of those sparks flying one to the other or from the ether.

Effective brainstorming is one of the easiest things to introduce, however harsh the cultural climate. In fact, some of our programmes are modular, project-based and spread over two separate weeks with a project day in between. Brainstorming is introduced in the first module. From experience, about half the managers have successfully introduced it back in the office by the second module, not only with the team which they lead, but also with the one where they are a team member.

In fact, effective group creativity is a rare species in our companies. Only about a third of managers attending the programmes I have been involved in say they use it. Of those, only about a third apply the rule. Finally, those that use brainstorming effectively have almost to a man (or woman) learnt it on a previous external programme, which leaves the vast pool from top decision-takers to supervisors out in the cold.

If we are going to deploy group creativity, we will need to explain why we are introducing it, set out the rule and the reason, and try to encourage a relaxed atmosphere. Also a separate room is a good idea, when introducing brainstorming, as it helps remove status and is itself a change from the norm. Flipcharts or white board will be needed so that there is a visual display of the ideas, or the group can stick post-it notes around the walls. In the former case, there will need to be a scribe, who is also a contributor. In the latter, the ideas should be verbally articulated as well as written down. In both cases, someone needs to ensure the no-criticism rule is followed.

We need not mention specific techniques like provocation, which can put a few people off. Such sophistications can come later to enhance the process. It will be so successful, and perceived as such by all, that brainstorming will become a way of life.

I finish off with a few benefits and a few things to avoid.

Benefits

- The creative output will be far higher than that of any individual. We all have our mindsets, our limited background, experience and knowledge. By opening our minds, sharing our ideas and allowing those sparks to be generated, we all become more creative and the whole always exceeds the sum of the individual parts.
- This holds also for evaluation. We can tap only into ourselves. The combined wealth of knowledge and experience of the group makes evaluation quicker and more effective.
- Fundamental improvements in work processes will occur. It can be applied to issue identification, problem solving, project definition, writing a scoping paper, planning and so on. It can be used for group work like defining and allocating key tasks and for individual tasks at any vital stage. Increasingly it becomes informal and swift. Other team members are happy to be involved for four reasons:
  — It improves the efficiency and effectiveness of a colleague's work.
  — As it is reciprocated, it improves the efficiency and effectiveness of their own work.
  — The knowledge of the group about each individual's key work activities expands enormously. This makes it much easier to take up the reins when a colleague is sick or on leave.
  — Team morale soars.
- It is the way to generate a shared vision, common understanding, agreed objectives and a sense of unity and direction.

Things to avoid

There are quite a number of pitfalls to avoid.

Number of ideas

The textbook definition of 'brainstorming' contains the instructions 'to generate as many ideas as possible within a finite time'. The result of believing this can be a focus on the means and not the end ie generating ideas rather than solving problems. There can be a machismo involved. 'In ten minutes, our group came up with 120 ideas – yours only managed 50.'

In fact one writer and practitioner, who shall remain nameless, proudly told his readers that, in one brainstorming, they had managed 100 'restatements' of the problem. Many of these were subject to further brainstorming, which led to thousands of ideas. These all needed evaluation. That took months!

That is why I suggest trying to limit crazy ideas to reversal or exaggeration approaches. Certainly, don't go for quantity for quantity's sake. The quality of ideas is much more important. There can be quite a pressure on the individual in the wrong environment. People feel guilty if there is silence or they have not contributed. Silence, a positive contemplation, can be the source of excellent ideas. We have no control, of course, as the no-criticism rule takes primacy – but we can affect the atmosphere and initial mind-set.

Numbers

The experts vary as to the right number. The minimum usually suggested is five and the maximum 12 or 20, depending on who you read. They acknowledge that the larger numbers lead to some individuals not contributing nor being part of the process. Presumably the atmosphere and the individual is sacrificed on the altar of quantity.

I see group creativity as a process involving a team (no more than 8, no less than 4) with a genuine work purpose and function, with all the benefits that reality brings.

Event

Brainstorming can be seen as a rare and major event, reserved for a major strategic issue, attended by a select group, usually off-site and expensive. There is a place for that, especially where the top team is involved. But it can give the wrong cultural messages – particularly that brainstorming is not a cheap, effective work-based, regular team activity.

Isolation

Brainstorming is sometimes carried out in isolation. Evaluation and implementation are done later, occasionally by different

people. Again, brainstorming should be an integrated part of problem-solving and action planning, where the same people switch out of creativity to logic, and back again, where necessary.
Such approaches have severe drawbacks.

- They can reinforce the cynical view that ideas are a waste of time. 'A lot of silly ideas, and no action.'
- They can be very time-consuming – and time is money. This creates resistance in many not in the cynical camp.
- If not part of normal work processes, but special events, they can reinforce or create a 'not invented here' mentality.

In fact, the wrong approach to brainstorming can encourage resistance to the use of creativity in the organisation as a whole!

8

◆ Facilitation ◆

We have looked at creativity and how we, as individuals and assertive persuaders, can become more creative and hence more effective. We have also considered how, by focusing on the group and introducing group creativity, we not only empower our team but also ourselves. Through both enhanced individual and group creativity, we are increasing our ability to be effective VTLs.

The leader of an effective brainstorm is the first cousin of a facilitator. A facilitator is not seen as a leader in conventional thinking. However, facilitation is at the heart of empowerment – a key skill of the VTL.

Reversal thinking is useful here. The characteristic of most leaders, because of upbringing, because of the historic role-model and because of status and positional power, is to be the voice that is heard much more frequently than any of her followers. As leaders, often not deliberately nor consciously, it is our views and our opinions, our ideas and our solutions that hold sway.

How could this reality be overturned? By not allowing us to express any views or opinions! A good facilitator has no views or opinions but enables the expression and discussion of the views and opinions of the group with whom he is carrying out his role.

Rather than talking about facilitation, I will exemplify it working in practice.

I have Thomas's permission to tell his tale. Some time ago, he attended one of our programmes. I met him afterwards occasionally for a pint and a chat, as he lived near the management centre, and I was very interested in his approach to facilitation.

Thomas is now a senior manager in a large company, but, at the time, was a middle manager – second in command of a section in a department of seventy staff.

BACKGROUND

His company, as many have, carried out a staff attitude survey. It was devised and administered by external consultants. The survey, in the form of a questionnaire, covered a wide range of issues, looking both externally and internally. The response rate was 50 per cent and the initial follow-up was a glossy brochure to outline the main findings. The next phase was a company-wide exercise where groups were to meet, discuss the key findings and implement agreed changes.

This process generally was very unsuccessful, because the leaders of the groups were the bosses. They were supposed to empower their groups, but had no training as facilitators – so adopted their normal leadership style. Equally, the internal issues, which came out of the survey as problem areas, were communication flows, motivation, poor delegation, lack of strategic direction and the like. If junior staff were honest about their own opinions on such matters, they would be directly criticising the bosses, asking them to discuss them! Political reality and cultural norms – the very norms the survey wanted to uncover and alter – took over. No right-minded junior dared to raise criticisms in front of her boss, responsible for her staff appraisal and promotion prospects, and in charge of the meeting!

A final problem was that the numbers attending each meeting (to save time) were between 10 and 12. Effective teams number no more than 8 and no less than 4. With 10 to 12 present, not everyone will contribute.

PLANNING AND PREPARATION

Now, Thomas's head of department was a very progressive and enlightened man. Thomas was a people-person, and recognised as such. With the recommendation of the personnel department behind him, he asked for and was given the authority to mastermind the feedback process.

The first step Thomas took was to ignore the survey! His customers were the departmental staff, and he wanted the agenda to be customer-driven. They had replied passively to pre-set questions. Additionally the only differentiation made in the survey was between managers and non-managers.

So, under the signature of the head of department, he sent out a positive up-beat letter, asking each member of staff to complete and return a non-attributable questionnaire. The questionnaire was simplicity itself. They were to write down what were the four most important work-related or 'local' problems they faced and any suggested solutions, and the four most important external or 'global' problems the company faced and suggested solutions. (In hindsight, Thomas realised that he should have achieved a balanced approach by also asking for successes and the reasons for them.) However, the survey focused on problems and set the tone, which he did not question at the time. Accentuating the positive as well as the negative is a more effective approach to staff-related issues.

Every company does some things well, and there is a danger of reducing morale by concentrating on problems. It is similar in the individual case. Everyone has strengths, and it is important for self-development and self-respect for these to be recognised, acknowledged and developed. The message should be: 'We are good, but we are going to be great!')

The final and very important detail was for the respondent to put a letter code in a box, which identified whether they were secretarial, junior clerical, senior clerical, officers, junior management, middle management or senior management.

The response rate was 70 per cent. This segmentation was necessary, as Thomas intended to run peer group meetings, and useful, as it showed the nature and extent of differences between levels. One that transpired in the meetings was that each level was happy with communication downwards (for which they were responsible) and most disgruntled with the communication received from the next level up!

Peer groups have a commonality of problems, and are more likely to open up if their boss isn't there – unless she is a VTL!

From the replies came the agendas, circulated in advance. Thomas also addressed logistics, arranging times (an hour and a half maximum), numbers between 4 and 8, a room outside the department, of the appropriate size, with the appropriate table and visual aids in the form of flipcharts and white-boards. Coffee, tea and biscuits were organised for all meetings.

Thomas also suppressed a video, which he was supposed to show to kick off each meeting, according to the official pack he had received. It was a bit of a disaster, Thomas told me. The skills displayed by the 'facilitating' boss were low, the level of interaction and the quality of discussion were low, and the issues raised or discussed varied from the mundane to the trivial. Thomas mentioned one that took up a significant part of the video time – the quality of toilet paper provided in the ladies' loos!

If the culture denies discussion of the important, and a discussion has to take place, then only the unimportant will surface.

Before each meeting, Thomas had used the flipcharts to write the headings for his introductory comments, as well as putting down the most important issues (in terms of questionnaire replies) in each category (local and global) and any solutions suggested.

He facilitated at eleven meetings – three secretarial, one junior clerical, one senior clerical, one officer, two junior management, two middle management and the final one – senior management. Thomas recalled wryly that, initially, the senior meeting was cancelled (pressure of work was the excuse). This was due to the natural reluctance of the section heads and head of department to appear before a junior in a kind of leadership role. However the outcry from below forced the head of department to change his mind, which was very courageous.

Thomas was a great success in his role. In fact Thomas confided in me that the grateful head of department, who reviewed the annual appraisal subsequently completed by his boss – a section head, had written on it 'Thomas has shown outstanding capabilities as a facilitator and communicator'. Now Thomas was not especially gifted, just a competent manager, as most of us are. It is worth examining what he did and why, to produce such an accolade. There is a clear route map we can all follow if we want to be able to empower our team.

The key success factors were:

- To set the objectives and ensure they were understood and agreed.
- To set expectations explicitly, gain agreement and ensure they were met.
- To set the rules of behaviour explicitly, gain agreement and ensure they were met.
- To ensure focus so that the business was completed on time.

A very interesting fact was that Thomas's approach was identical for every meeting and successful at every meeting. Remember we are taking a range from secretary to executive head. Empowerment is, in fact, not as hard as we might think.

Thomas had the courage to try what was a culturally radical approach, because of the dimensions of the problems he knew he faced. Most of his customers were sceptical and many were cynical. Being a large company, with years of success until the winds of change blew into a gale, it was still locked into a culture where behaviours accorded to established norms, based on hierarchy, status, conformity and the individual. Such environments are the breeding ground for scepticism and cynicism! Also, as the process was a first, there was a high degree of uncertainty and discomfort.

There was a measure of resentment from his peers, seeing Thomas in a lead role, and his seniors did not want to be there!

THE MEETING

Thomas knew that what he said to begin the meeting would have an enormous impact on the outcome. I paraphrase the comments Thomas made, as he was kind enough to give me a note of his approach, which he had written up after the event. He spoke for nearly five minutes, running through each heading on the flipchart, as follows:

Opportunity

Members at the meeting were not often provided with an opportunity to improve their working environment and they were encouraged to take full advantage of it. Thomas saw this as a positive emphasis of how important the meeting was.

The problems

It was recognised that some people might not identify with the problems on the agenda. It was hoped that they would, nevertheless, try to be interested in these problems and be involved in the search for effective solutions. It was also pointed out that:

- Their problems might be raised at another meeting.
- As the meeting progressed, the definition of problems on the agenda might change.
- There might be time for consideration of problems specific to individuals at the end of the meeting, if they had not been covered.

Thomas had recognised that, with nearly 100 per cent attendance at the meetings, and only a 70 per cent questionnaire response (20 per cent less cynical than the survey!), some individuals' problems would not be on the agenda. Equally, the necessity to prioritise the problems and take the top six or so shared by most meant that specific issues had fallen by the wayside. He felt that this reality had to be faced up-front initially.

However, nearly all identified with the top few problems such as poor communications both within and between sections, duplication of work and effort, poor management of workflows, and ineffective use of IT systems, as all were affected by them.

Equal worth

It was pointed out that some individuals felt that their opinions and views were more important than anyone else's and conversely a few individuals felt that their views were less significant. At this meeting every individual had equal worth and so the facilitator would try to ensure that they had equal time to express their views. It was hoped that individuals would show mutual respect and any comments on other people's views would be polite and constructive.

This was a core component of success. Thomas, though it would not be the language he would use, had set out what we could call explicit equality rules of behaviour to generate the desired positive outcomes.

If the assertive persuader or VTL has a respect for herself, and an equal respect for her colleagues, then, whether implicitly or not, she will be encouraging and adopting equality rules of behaviour. What is worthy of particular note is how setting this out explicitly can create new group norms and new behaviours.

The role of facilitator

It was explained that the role of facilitator was simply to make the meeting run easily. To this end, the facilitator would:

- Encourage a friendly atmosphere.
- Ensure that objectivity was maintained eg there was no degeneration into personalities/grievances nor identifying individuals. Any 'personal' problem could be expressed in general terms.
- Ensure effective time-keeping. It was hoped that all problems would be covered, but if the debate on local issues carried on, the facilitator would be reluctant to close it down and would be prepared to sacrifice global problems.

  Thomas mentioned to me that, in most instances, that is exactly what happened. This was not surprising as staff tend to be more interested in the issues involving their working environment than issues relating to the company's relationship with its external business environment.
- Ensure that one rule was maintained throughout the meeting ie all comments should be expressed through the facilitator as this would avoid meetings within meetings or comments becoming too personal.
- Would not have any opinions himself, unusual for this particular facilitator! It was their problems and their meeting and it was not for the facilitator to introduce or impose his own views.

  This is a critical rule for an effective facilitator and, Thomas told me, the remark invariably produced a laugh, as Thomas was noted for the range of his opinions and the frequency with which he expressed them! Indeed, Thomas also told me, when we were discussing this over a pint or two, that the head of department mentioned to him his amazement that Thomas had kept to the rule.

Thomas told me that it had not been difficult. If we take on a role, prepare for it, and the structure and rules are at the forefront of our minds, it is remarkably easy to accept the discipline and enjoy the rewards that discipline brings. The brainstorming rule is another example.

His problem, he told me, occurred at the second or third meeting of the same level of staff, where he knew the answers from the previous deliberations and had to keep quiet, when inferior solutions were being put forward and accepted.

■ Would, however, act as a catalyst to develop thinking where blind alleys or cul-de-sacs had occurred. Thomas felt that this was necessary to keep momentum going. He rarely had to intervene, and interventions were not his own views, but suggestions of alternatives or new avenues that might fruitfully be explored.

The overall approach and the question of consensus

On one flipchart, all the problems had already been set out, one per page. There was a 'D' symbol where the dimensions of the problem could be developed, specific instances mentioned, the importance considered etc, if this was required.

On the other flipchart there was an 'S' entry for the solutions and 'I' entry for implementation issues. Thomas told me that implementation aspects were rarely covered because of the reality that the power of implementation lay elsewhere.

As regards consensus, it was pointed out that there would be no drive for consensus. If it occurred, that was excellent but a majority, minority or equality of opinions on problems or solutions was quite acceptable. It was hoped that, as each would be considered, the group as a whole could consider them even if it was not the problem or solution of some individuals.

Thomas mentioned that, in fact, there was a high degree of consensus on the solution paths (containing more than one idea or 'one right answer') that emerged, but minority views were expressed, occasionally maintained after the subsequent debate, and duly recorded.

Minutes

The facilitator would record the key points. For the sake of efficiency, if it was acceptable to everyone, one member attending would examine the draft on behalf of the other members and make the necessary changes, after which they would be sent out.

Thomas found this role quite easy, as he could produce them from the flipcharts he filled in during the meeting. Thomas felt that if a member attending had been fingered for the role, that would deny her effective involvement during the meeting.

Equally, if some junior member of staff had been brought in for the purpose, she would not be part of the discussion and would act unwittingly as a constraint on the generation of the open, involved atmosphere he desired.

By having only one person vetting the minutes, he could get them out quickly.

Where do we go from here?

It was pointed out that a complete report would be submitted to the head of department and the section heads, who would meet to decide on implementation.

Any comments

At the end of his introductory remarks, Thomas asked for comments and agreement to the approach, structure and rules. Thomas advised me that there were no comments at any meeting and always verbal agreement.

This is a key aspect. While most present, no doubt, genuinely agreed, one or two may well have been unhappy with certain aspects. However, it would not have looked good to express their feelings.

So they kept quiet, and thereby gave the facilitator the power he needed to ensure that what happened subsequently accorded with what he wanted to happen.

'That's very interesting, John, but we have not heard from Julie yet, and, as you know, we are making sure that everyone has the opportunity to express their views. Julie, what do you think about formal meetings at peer group level between the sections?'

'Charles, please remember to address your comments through me.'

'Victoria, that comment is a bit personal. Remember, please, to talk in general terms. What you are saying – and correct me if I am wrong – is that the junior manager in your section does not hold any team meetings of clerical staff to improve the communication flow. Does anyone else have the same problem?'

Thomas had, unwittingly, replaced the negative power of the implicit by the positive power of the explicit, and changed behaviour (even if only at those meetings) as a result.

OUTCOMES

Short-term

The exercise was an undoubted success, as the general and individual feedback to Thomas proved. Real staff issues had been raised and discussed, and effective solutions put forward. Invariably a positive brainstorming, problem-solving approach had resulted. The individual left the meeting in the happy knowledge that her voice had been heard, and ideas listened to. Ideas had been shared, common attitudes exposed and consensus solutions developed.

The outcome was, as we have seen, positive for Thomas.

Long-term

The picture became much less rosy. Thomas advised me that the top team in the department were only really interested in looking up and not down, because of the cultural norms. In fact, after prodding the head of department, he wrote for him a mild and unattributable document, setting out the areas of improvement, suggested for the top executives! This had been the focus of their discussions, as the section heads could hardly criticise their boss, who was at the meeting! The memo was duly sent and ignored.

There was no momentum behind implementation, and Thomas found himself attending implementation meetings in a junior, subordinate role with endless excuses being found by his 'superiors' to defer and diminish the problems addressed and solutions implemented. He had become a powerless vox populi – ' voice of the people '.

During this protracted period of vacillation and diminution, the head of department was promoted and replaced by an individual even less concerned with people issues – end of story.

As Thomas said to me:

'At the end of the day, I did the department a singular disservice. If I hadn't interfered with the normal process, expectations would not have been raised, everyone would have just gone through the motions as the culture dictated, and no real damage would have been done.'

In fact, he told me that, because of his role, he had been able to read the much more detailed findings of the survey (not for public dissemination, because it included such gems as the fact that the vast majority of managers said that it did not pay to stick their heads above the parapet!). He had discovered that the generally negative survey findings mirrored those of a similar survey 11 years previously. No doubt, there had been an equally ineffective follow-up at that time!

Thomas, unwittingly, had raised expectations, subsequently dashed them and therefore reduced morale.

Specific

There was a specific, beneficial outcome. A year or two later, Thomas was asked to chair a steering committee.

What he did was to adopt the vast majority of the approaches and skills he had deployed as facilitator in his new role.

The fundamental difference was that he was allowed to have opinions. However, by using the brainstorming, open and explicit approach, his opinions became part of the idea generation or were put forward into an environment of genuine debate, where the views of others were considered and respected.

At the end of the day, many of his views were adopted, some were rejected but most were part of the emerging consensus and were formulated at the meeting and not in advance.

The other difference was that he was in a genuine leadership role! As leaders, we can always empower our followers, whatever the culture. If there are enough of us, we can empower the company over time – change culture. If the managing director becomes a VTL, it takes less time!

In a world of change, time is short.

So, armed with the knowledge about the key skills required, first to become assertive persuaders and second VTLs, what next?

Next, we look at the critical event in the persuasion context – the persuasion meeting, focusing on the primary relationship considered in this book – the one-to-one relationship.

9

◆ The Persuasion Meeting ◆

In this chapter we consider the many occasions when we are in the role of persuader or persuadee, and a future time has been agreed for a meeting to take place between the two individuals. We will concentrate on the role of persuader, though clearly the approach will be useful when we are going to be persuaded and know in advance what the subject matter is.

Often there is not a clear separation of roles. Indeed, the development of harmony and consensus will remove what initial distinction there was – no longer persuasion, but co-operation.

Examples are:

- An annual appraisal with the boss.
- A specific meeting with the boss to ask for promotion, a pay rise or a transfer.
- A new project, which requires the boss's approval.
- An important meeting with a client to whom we want to sell a product or service.
- Persuading a colleague to join a project team.
- Interviewing for a job in our section/team.
- Off-the-record chat with a subordinate whose performance has slipped.

We should take advantage of the precious gift of time before the persuasion meeting occurs.

Some key thoughts follow.

MAXIMISE THE INFORMATION BASE

We need to establish as many facts as possible, rather than just opinions.

As assertive persuaders, we will expand our information base early on during the actual meeting, but we should take full advantage of the opportunity offered beforehand.

Take the example of John, the man who was more than
half-an-hour late. EP held his own opinions as facts, and did not
bother finding out, before or during, any facts relating to John,
other than those provided by his junior manager. AP had
established in advance three facts, not shared by EP.

- John's lateness was atypical – had only occurred that week.
- The traffic conditions on John's route were normal.
- John was leaving work at the normal time. (If he had found out
  that John was making up the time lost in the morning by
  working later in the evening, and assuming this was OK, the
  discussion might not have taken place.)

These facts were of considerable benefit to AP.

However, it is not only facts we should investigate, but also the
persuadee's feelings and attitudes, where the individual concerned is known to us – the norm in the work environment. I shall
develop this aspect under the section Consider the Approach.

SET THE OBJECTIVE

If we have no target, we cannot aim the rifle. We need to decide in
advance what we want from the meeting – what our objective is.
Some very major issues are rarely decided by one meeting. It can
take months, if not years, before a relationship with a prospective
client is sufficiently well developed for the business to flow and/or
the switch from our competitor to take place. If we go in cold, and
expect a million pounds worth of orders from one meeting, we will
disappointed. More importantly, the way we have conducted
ourselves with the prospective client may guarantee that disappointment is permanent!

Equally, if our boss has no inkling that we want a transfer or
promotion, we should not expect his agreement as the result of an
half-an-hour chat. If we make that our objective, we are likely to be
very disappointed. And who will we blame? Just ourselves or our
boss as well? And what happens to our relationship with our boss,
if we blame him? And, as he is our boss, what happens to our
career?

The reverse holds. If we want our subordinate to do something,
for which he is totally unprepared, do we expect a yes or no (or
perhaps just a yes!) before he is psychologically ready ie capable of
being persuaded?

So, we must not be too ambitious. If the boss is cold, perhaps our
objectives should be to get her to think about it *and* to have agreed

the time of the next meeting. However, if this meeting is a 'warm' meeting, when we have already done the spadework, then the ultimate goal can be the actual objective of that meeting.

We begin to see that the very act of recognising the need for an explicit objective is increasing the probability of success.

CONSIDER THE APPROACH

Having set our objective or objectives, we need to consider what our overall approach should be. There are three related aspects – Game Theory, Perceived Balance of Advantage (PBA) and Flexibility.

Game theory

Many of you will be familiar with Game Theory, and you may have picked up on my references in earlier chapters to win/win outcomes.

The classic example is 'The Prisoners' Dilemma'. Two prisoners are believed to have committed a murder together, and have been caught and put into a prison. Neither has confessed. The governor of the prison is interested in getting a confession. He doesn't care which confesses or whether both confess, as long as he gets a confession, which will make him look good. For the purposes of this 'game', the governor is a *deus ex machina* ie policeman, judge, jury and executioner rolled into one.

The governor talks to each prisoner separately. He says to each prisoner, 'If you confess to the murder and your partner in crime does not, you will be set free, and he will be hung. If neither of you confess, you will both be freed without reward. If both of you confess, you will each receive a ten-year jail sentence. Think about it overnight, and tell me your decision in the morning.'

What would you say to the governor in the morning?
Specifically:

1. What will be the outcome, if the prisoners cannot talk to each other?

2. What will be the outcome if the prisoners can talk to each other, and trust each other?

3. What will be the incentive for a prisoner to break the agreement?

The answers are:

	No communication or communication and no trust	Communication with trust	Communication agreement and betrayal 1	Communication agreement and betrayal 2
Prisoner 1	**L** 10 years in jail	**W** Freed	**W** Freed with reward	**L** Hung
Prisoner 2	**L** 10 years in jail	**W** Freed	**L** Hung	**W** Freed with reward

Figure 44 Outcomes of Prisoners' Dilemmas

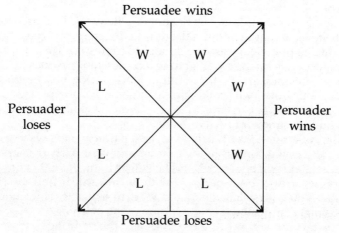

Figure 45 Outcomes from persuasion situation

1. Each will confess and go to jail for ten years. They do not know what the other will say. They do know that if the other confesses, and they stay silent, they will hang. That risk is too great. As the governor knew, if the prisoners were kept apart, he won and they lost.

2. However, they were both expert at Morse code, and they were in adjacent cells, or they could shout and be heard, or the

governor was careless and allowed them to slop out or eat together in the morning. If they talked and trusted, they would not confess and go free. United, they won, and the governor lost.

3. There is no honour among murderers. One broke his agreement, confessed and not only went free, but with a nice reward. His fellow prisoner was hung.

Finally, if both prisoners pretended trust, and broke it by confessing, they are back to square one – in jail for ten years. I have put these outcomes on a matrix, set out in Figure 44.

Instead of prisoners, we could think of persuader and persuadee. Instead of life or death, we could think of the possible outcomes of the persuasion situation. These outcomes have been set out, in Figure 45, in the conventional game theory matrix, where each quadrant produces a combination of win and lose. They run from lose/lose through to win/win. It's worth considering each one in turn.

Lose/lose

This could be the clash of EPs, where there is equality of status and a complete breakdown. The interaction produces maximum heat and minimum light. There is no movement from initial positions, no change in perception, and no ability or interest in understanding the persuadee, a reality that is reciprocated.

At a more subtle level, the outcome could be where both agree to do something the other wants, and neither follows through.

The setting of false expectations, subsequently shattered, ensures a poor relationship deteriorates. It sounds implausible, but it does happen. For instance, two functional directors, both strong in Logic and Incentives put under pressure by the managing director to sort out their differences, operating in a culture where superficial politeness is the norm.

Win/lose

The persuader wins and the persuadee loses. The case of John with EP is an example. Aggressive persuaders (high in Logic and Incentives) with positional power to reinforce their persuasion approach usually achieve these outcomes with subordinates.

There is a perception operating both at societal and individual level that aggression pays. Often it is implicitly rather than explicitly believed. There are, however, two fundamental drawbacks. From a relationship point of view, the quality of relationships 'enjoyed' by the aggressive persuader is poor. From a business point of view, there is a loss of value. The win/win outcome produces maximum value from the interaction. Any other outcome produces waste.

The learning curve that managers ascend in this area is very interesting, when they are attending an appropriate and effective programme. If the dynamics of the course go the way they should, the perception develops in all of the value from positive, productive one-to-one and team interactions. By the end of the second module, when team cohesion is at its height, we often introduce a game called 'Counterplay'. Each team is provided with five tiddleywinks of a different colour. The objective of the game is to maximise points. Points are given at the end of each round after a period of negotiation between teams to try to obtain tiddleywinks of the same colour. The highest points are awarded for five tiddleywinks of the same colour, the next highest for four of the same colour and so on. Bonus points are awarded each round to any team that is the clear winner of the round and penalty points if any rules are infringed such as trading in the planning period or failing to hand in the tiddleywinks to the umpire on time. There are five rounds with random distributions of tiddleywinks for the last four rounds.

It is fast and furious and the whole gamut of human behaviour passes before our eyes. If one team pulls ahead early on, the others invariably gang up on it to pull it back into the pack.

There is a detailed debrief afterwards where, among many other things, ethics are considered! Intra-team cohesion tends to be maintained, but inter-team rivalry is intense – hence the need to consider ethics in the light of actual behaviour.

Value is never maximised for two reasons. There is no strategy developed to maximise value. There is a strategy to destroy it. It never crosses anyone's mind that they should and could maximise value by co-operation between teams. Every team's point score would be significantly enhanced by such co-operation, and the 'winner' determined by the luck from the random distribution, coupled with the application of the method to achieve maximum value. Of course, with that approach there would be no perception of a winner, as each team and each individual would have won. The connection to the real world is powerfully made, when the interactions between production, selling, marketing and such-like 'teams' are considered by the managers.

Most companies in the world of change they live in want to maximise value to customers. Most are striving for a common vision and mission to act as the catalyst for that value. Few recognise the need for effective persuasion skills to be developed at the individual and group levels to achieve the reality.

A final point. The aggressive winner may win in time, but usually loses over time.

Lose/win

The persuader loses and the persuadee wins. For instance, the persuader is the subordinate, and either he is non-assertive or aggressive with an aggressive boss, and has to yield to positional power. Alternatively, we can have the submissive boss as the persuader with an aggressive or manipulative subordinate as the persuadee.

Win/win

If we go back to the example of the Prisoners' Dilemma, we will notice that the value of the win is greater when the other prisoner loses than when they both win. The overall value is, however, less then that achieved by the win/win outcome.

The Prisoners' Dilemma is an exercise in logic, with a number of immutable constraints. Hence, the smack of compromise that a purely logical approach delivers.

If trust is generated and creativity deployed, the shared victory has a greater value for both individuals than by winning at the expense of the other.

So what should we aim for? We should aim for the win/win. As we have seen in earlier chapters, if we intend for this to be our approach, we need to understand where the persuadee is coming from, what makes her tick. We have to be assertive persuaders.

I am reminded of this very forcefully by a role play carried out nearly two years ago between two managers on our senior executive programme. I cannot remember all the details, but it was a dry run for a real life interview that was scheduled to take place soon after the persuader was due back in his company. It was particularly interesting because the persuadee played the role of the boss.

The first attempt was a disaster. The persuader was rather full of himself, very strong on the benefits to the customer and the company, which he assumed would be clinchers, and occasionally was verbally aggressive. This was despite the fact that he had briefed the persuadee as to the main characteristics of his boss, which included empire building, personal prestige and a dislike of major change. The project, as presented, represented major change, reduced his boss's empire, and what came out was how good it would be for the persuader!. The person playing the role of persuadee – the boss – played it well, but it was not difficult.

All five of us had a chat. (There were two other managers acting as observers and commentators until it was their turn.) Then the two individuals replayed it with the persuader having a completely different approach, which at the time was successful. I was advised by the persuader months later that it took a few interviews, but the project was set up with only minor changes.

What we discussed was Perceived Balance of Advantage (PBA).

Perceived balance of advantage

This is a very simple and powerful concept. During any stage of a persuasion situation, if the persuadee perceives that there is a balance of advantage for her in the proposition, she will accept it. There are two implications:

1. We, in the role of persuaders, should try to stand in the shoes of the persuadee, and, in advance of the meeting, have identified what he will perceive as a positive or negative aspect of the proposition. We should start the main discussion with some positives and accentuate them to generate momentum, mention but minimise the negatives, and keep a positive up the sleeve, to be used if and when necessary. This strategy will maximise our chances of success.

   If it is a meeting with a stranger, we should use our empathy skills to adopt the same approach at the meeting. Equally, if these aspects can be identified in advance, we should not assume they are cast in concrete, but use our questioning and listening skills to pick up where changed reality necessitates a change in our perceptions.

   This is what happened in the revised role play. The persuader highlighted how the increased client satisfaction and corporate benefits would significantly enhance his boss's reputation, how a dotted reporting line could be maintained so that his empire would be seen to expand, and played down the extent and pace of change. This was done reasonably subtly!

2. We must recognise when we have won! This PBA can come quickly, and often comes before we have finished. This is why we have to be perceptive and not menu-driven. Sometimes we succeed, when we are not prepared to accept success! That can lead to subsequent failure. I have seen it so often. The persuadee indicates agreement. The persuader does not seize the moment and close down to action-planning, but carries on. A change in mood, a different slant, another issue being raised

that turns the meeting sour – and all is lost. What can also happen is that there is agreement to part of the proposition, but again that is not closed down and out of subsequent debate. The same fate often awaits.

Flexibility

Implicit in the above is the need to be flexible. As stated, we can lose if we are menu-driven, and do not seize the moment. We can lose if we focus on our initial objective, to the exclusion of the messages that the persuadee transmits. We must be flexible, which is one reason we need to develop effective listening skills. Mentally, as an integral part of our preparation, we should 'think flexible' as well as 'think win/win' and 'think persuadee'. There is another reason.

Time for a story a colleague of mine tells to course members. Nazaruddin has some valuable carpets to sell in the marketplace. He spends the day in skilful negotiations with prospective purchasers. At the end of the day he meets his friend for a few drinks. Nazaruddin's hands are empty and his pockets jangle with the weight of silver in them. He is flushed with excitement and feelings of victory and triumph. 'I have done it', he cries. 'I have done it. This is the best day of my life. My objective was twenty pieces of silver and I made forty. O frabjous day! Callooh! Callay! (Nazaruddin was well read and had been a manager in a former life!)

To which his friend replied with melancholy mien: 'But Nazaruddin. Those carpets were the most beautiful and valuable I have ever seen. You should have got far far more than forty pieces of silver. You should have got forty pieces of **GOLD**!'

Nazaruddin said: 'What is this gold?'

We are limited by our knowledge, which determines our horizons. If we are flexible and have open ears, we can change both.

CONSIDER THE STRUCTURE OF THE MEETING

We should consider in advance how we should structure the meeting. While most of us are aware of the main flow, there can be one or two aspects that will elude our attention, unless we think about them in advance and have planned our strategy.

Physical arrangement

Do we sit behind a desk – a barrier and a comfort? Do we sit fairly close with empty space between us? Do we have a low coffee table or high work table? How far apart should we be?

Received wisdom is that there should be no inequality of status (farewell, imposing desk), no physical barrier (farewell, high table), respect for personal space (chairs not too close), and not directly facing (avoids eyeballing but permits direct eye contact when appropriate). Low table is fine. This sort of approach is increasingly becoming the norm, and increasingly the coffee table is disappearing. However, there are many exceptions, partly deliberately and partly through lack of training. There is another facet as well. Situations often arise when the physical arrangement is such as to maximise the potential for effective persuasion, but the subsequent meeting fails to achieve it. Some bosses with a high internal focus have yielded to the new approach and moved from behind their desks, but in the absence of any training or commitment to training provided, proceed in their normal fashion. I have come across it quite often, and the body language alone is a give-away, as they strain to put as much distance as possible between themselves with no protection and the persuadee uncomfortably close.

Introductions

It is important we set the persuadee at her ease. The standard pleasantries play a necessary part in this process, but we should not overdo them and suffer the perception of artificiality. A smile is worth a thousand words.

The agenda

Should we be explicit or not? Should we set out our objective(s) and reasons for them up front and gain agreement to consider them? I ask because so many persuaders do not. I remember one recently on a senior executive programme. This was a real problem and the role-play a dry run for the real thing. The persuader (let us call him Paul) was the production director in a brewery. One of his staff had an alcohol problem! Drinking was not allowed on the premises, and the individual concerned (say George) had not been caught breaching the rule. However, he did turn up for work stinking of drink, his performance was satisfactory but deteriorating. He had lost all his former sparkle and his wife had approached the foreman asking for his support in getting her husband to face up to reality and seek counselling. The foreman had tried his best, but George would not admit he had a problem. As a result Paul had been asked by the foreman to deal with the matter.

I must say, as an aside, we get some really tough problems, and some fascinating insights into attitudes and prejudices.

What was interesting was that Paul's approach was completely tangential. The reason given for the meeting was that it was just a chat, which Paul was having with many others. The subject of drinking was introduced without explanation halfway through. Concern was expressed on whether drinking might be affecting George's performance without any statement that it was. A large chunk of time was devoted to trying to find out how many drinks George had before his shifts, and whether this was normal. George was a skilled thespian and the meeting finished without agreement or way forward.

It was a very tough problem, riddled with legal issues, the question of evidence, and whether a manager should get involved in psychological aspects without training or experience. Incidentally, the decision taken by Paul in the light of the group discussions was to involve a personnel officer, qualified in psychology.

Paul did not agree with the direct approach, I think wisely in this case. He was treading dangerous waters, and had recognised this.

Does the exception prove the rule? As assertive persuaders, we need to set expectations explicitly and early. An integral part of this process is to set out our objective and reason, but in a manner that takes into account the position of the persuadee.

Discussion

It is during the meat of the meeting – the discussion period – that our assertive persuasion skills come to the fore. Establishing facts, selling benefits from the perception of the persuadee (not ourselves), open questioning, listening, observing and reacting to body language. Ears open, flexible thinking, rational logic and empathy moving towards win/win.

Review

Periodically it is important that we review progress, make sure that both parties know what has been agreed to and why, just in case, as can happen so often, we are running down one track and the persuadee is walking down another!

Close

We will sense how far we can go at one meeting. If we have

achieved our objective for that meeting or even more, we must confirm the decisions agreed, agree the actions to be taken by whom and when, and set the date for the next meeting, where necessary.

Reality means that we will not always achieve the magic win/win. We need to close with what we can get, and not prolong matters so that we get less than we could.

Winning for the persuader or persuadee is often a matter of time and change in perception. Consider George and Paul. If Paul had persuaded George to seek professional help, Paul would have achieved his objective. I doubt George would have thought he was a winner with that outcome. If he successfully dried out, and professional help was the necessary first step, he would look back to that winning first step, and recognise it as such.

It reminds me of a pre-set role play, where a marketing director has to persuade her peer, the finance director, to sack one of his subordinates, an incompetent IT manager. The manager was a personal friend of the finance director and appointed by him. The individual playing the marketing director was one of the most effective persuaders I have come across, with the deployment, through questioning and listening skills, of rational logic and empathy.

She changed the objective to solving the IT problem rather than sacking the IT manager, which was very neat. She gained the finance director's commitment to an action plan which, in the absence of significant improvement by the IT manager, would put that individual's job at risk, but not obviously so – that reality would unwind.

In the debrief, the individual playing the finance director, the persuadee, was full of admiration for the persuader. He admitted that he had lost the encounter. That perception began to change, when it was pointed out that if he had successfully resisted any action (his concept of victory), and had allowed the situation to continue, he would lose standing with the managing director, might well find his hand forced, with considerable negative consequences for any promotion or power development.

He had in fact won, without knowing it – as the action plan permitted the opportunity for his friend to improve with training and support, and a logical rational process for his friend's departure, if it became necessary. Equally, in selling on to his friend he could not only resort to evidence but agreement with another – the marketing director.

Changing perception changes reality.

10

◆ The Case Study ◆

INTRODUCTION

This is the penultimate chapter. The last chapter examines how we can achieve real measurable improvements in those areas where we have determined we should and could improve our capabilities as effective persuaders.

Before doing so, we examine a real-life role-play in detail, and try to answer relevant questions on the actual persuasion interview and the competence and effectiveness of the two participants. We use the knowledge we have built up in the previous chapters, particularly the last.

The purpose is to provide a perspective on practice, to get a feel of what to do and what to avoid, and how we can be more effective when operating in the real business world rather than from the printed page.

BACKGROUND

You may well be asking what on earth the phrase 'real-life role-play' actually means. That is a good open question! Two managers, attending a leadership programme at Sundridge Park Management Centre, are playing the role of persuader and persuadee. They have had relevant input on persuasion and have had time to consider a situation that is real to the persuader. For the particular case study chosen, Colin – the persuader – has an ongoing problem with another member of staff – John. This is a major business issue for Colin, and the roleplay provides him with a dummy run before returning to the office to tackle the real John and try to resolve the issue satisfactorily. John, the persuadee, has been briefed by Colin as to the characteristics and approach he should display. One reason I have chosen this roleplay is that John played the part true to life, as Colin acknowledged afterwards.

Incidentally, this was often the case. There seem to be a lot of budding actors among our managers and executives!

I do not intend to provide any detail, but simply unwind the script, which paints a complete picture.

THE ROLE PLAY

As the camera begins to roll, Colin is already seated in a comfortable office chair. Colin has placed another similar chair about three feet away, with no barriers between the chairs – not even a low table. The chairs are only a few degrees from being face to face. When John has sat down, their feet are only about eighteen inches apart. Colin, at the beginning, is leaning back with his right leg crossed over the other at the top of the knee. This leg forms a horizontal plane on which Colin rests a clipboard. His right hand clasps the board, and his left is underneath it.

John, when sitting, has his legs crossed, but at the ankle. He is leaning back as well, but his head and neck are forward. He is holding a piece of paper with his right hand, his left hand (nearest the camera) is supporting his chin, with one finger pointing towards his ear, and the elbow resting on an arm of the chair. His head is inclined slightly to the side, supported by the left hand.

Colin: Thank you John. (As John comes in and sits down in the chair available.)

John: Morning Colin.

Colin: (Glances up briefly from his clipboard at John, then looks down and commences.) I'd like to run through a letter a client has sent to us. You've had it nearly three weeks, and I see you've not made any response yet. Can you tell me why that is? (Colin has continued to look down at his clipboard, but looks directly at John when posing the question.)

John: (When starting his reply, gently strokes the lobe of his left ear with his left hand, and does not look directly at Colin.) Well three weeks is not a very long time and, you know, Colin, I'll get round to it soon. It's at the top of my in-tray. (John gestures expansively with his left hand towards an imaginary in-tray and looks directly at Colin as he finishes.)

Colin: Are you aware that … well, you are aware that we haven't had any payments from this client for nearly six months? (Again, Colin starts by looking down at his clipboard, and finishes by looking directly at John.)

John: No, I wasn't aware of that. No, no! (When Colin had been speaking, John had been in a listening mode. Legs were still slightly crossed, both arms resting on the sides of the chair, head and neck leaning forward with head to one side and looking directly at Colin, catching his gaze when Colin looked up from his clipboard. When John replied, he fingered his left lobe again, shuffled his feet slightly, then returned to listening mode.)

Colin: And it's purely due to the information they have been waiting for. Obviously it has a detrimental effect on our cash-flow, something we are very concerned about, and also we are coming to the end of the client's financial year. (Colin looks up from clipboard directly at John, who is now supporting his chin with his left hand and is nodding vigorously.) That, basically, is probably the best time to finalise the account. I'd like to discuss with you (Colin, who has maintained a static body posture, as described at the beginning, except that both hands are underneath the clipboard now, makes a small open gesture with his right hand at this point, before replacing it under the board) how we can forward the information as quickly as possible and if there are any problems or sticking points which are preventing it.

John: Well, I think they are a rather pernickety client, and I don't think they are being perfectly square with us. You know we presented the invoice. (John leans forward from shoulder up, looks directly at Colin and gestures with his left hand.) I understand they want to see all sorts of other stuff, accounts and reports and the like and that's pretty unusual. Can't really understand why they don't just pay up. (There is a little cluster here. John shuffles his feet slightly, raises and lowers one foot, takes his left hand off his chin, plays with his lower lip with the fingers of his right hand and moves his head from side to side.) They're creating an awful lot of work for us.

Colin: Er, it is their money after all and they're quite entitled
to our co-operation. I think the important thing is
that we are looking at a small portion of the account,
which is preventing the account being settled. (John
murmurs agreement. Colin moves his left hand from
under the board to the top of the knee, as he
continues.) They are unwilling to consider the claim
you presented (looks directly at John) because they
have not received the information they requested in
their letter. I would like us to satisfy their
requirements.

John: (with expansive gestures with both hands) I am very
happy to furnish the information, Colin. I'll do that.
It's in my in-tray. (Looks round and gestures to
imaginary in-tray.) You know I'll do it. No problem.
(Direct look and little nods.)

Colin: I think we need to place a bit more urgency on it.
We're looking at about three months until the end of
their financial year.

John: (interrupts, leaning forward) Oh, I'll get it done by
then. (Nods head.) Don't worry about that. That's no
problem. (Stops nodding head, and moves it slightly
from side to side, eyes turned away from Colin to
look to the side, with a little throwaway gesture
with right hand.)

Colin: They need a lot of time to look at the work you are
presenting to them (John murmurs agreement) and,
em, they will need possibly close on a month to
negotiate the claim. So that'll give you about four
weeks. Do you think that's reasonable to present all
the information they require? (Colin looks up at the
end as usual, and apart from little spasmodic
gestures with left hand keeps legs crossed, clipboard
on lap, hands under the board and leans back and
away from John.)

John: It might be. I'll do my level best, Colin – but you know
(leans forward, open gesture with left hand) my
views on them as a client, Colin. (Hands moving to
open position on lap.) They're pretty pernickety –
one of the reasons for the delays is that they want all
of the "i"s dotted and the "t"s crossed. But I'll do
my best, Colin, I'll do my best. (Vigorous nodding.)

Colin: They are a very valuable client. If the account stays unsettled for a long time, it prevents us picking up more work. So, again, we are very concerned. (Direct look at John.) I think we need more of a commitment. We need to set some goals. (John murmurs agreement, pauses a little while with left hand on chin with the elbow supported by the right hand – in reflective mode.)

John: So you are a little bit worried that I am actually going to get it done on time?

Colin   (nods slightly) Yes, very concerned. (John murmurs and nods, looks directly at Colin, but says nothing. Colin pauses, looks away from John and back down to his clipboard and, hesitatingly) Do you think four weeks is unrealistic?

John: I think I ought to be able to do it in that time. (Nods and meets Colin's gaze, as he looks up from his clipboard.) Um, supposing I have any problems (gestures with his left hand), should I come and see you about it? Perhaps lay off doing other things, do you think? (Throw away gesture with left hand.)

Colin: I will quite willingly discuss this with you and help you where possible. As regards laying off other work (looks down), it's apparent, it should be apparent to you (direct look) that you've not got that much on at the moment. (Slight move forward of the chin.) That's been, well, that's been fairly well planned in order to release you to finalise the account. You may be aware that others in the office are under considerable pressure. What we'd like to do, once the account is settled, is obviously for you to pick up more work.

John: More work? (The vocal pitch rises significantly.)

Colin: So you see that it's very important that we have some commitment and wrap it up very quickly.

John: (nods) I'll do my best.

Colin: Can we set some timescale on it? (Direct look.)

John   (leans forward, nodding): Yes, OK. What did you have in mind?

Colin:	Can we say that we can present them with the majority of the information within three weeks? What I would also like us to do is to reply to their letter, which has been on file for nearly three weeks, and give them an indication as to when they can expect the information.
John:	Yea, OK (nodding.)
Colin:	You think that's agreeable?
John:	Well, I'll try to do it.
Colin:	I think we need to set those as targets and maybe review them in a couple of weeks' time, and see how we're getting on.
John:	OK (nods.)
Colin:	That's acceptable?
John:	Yes, it is. (End.)

ANALYSIS

There is a wealth of learning contained in this case study, not exclusively in the area of persuasion. Some aspects of management are included. What I would like you to do is spend a little time considering your answers to a few relevant questions before we consider together what are the key messages that can be uncovered.

So here are the questions:

■   What were the roles of Colin and John? Were they peers, or was one the boss and the other the subordinate? If so, who was who?

■   What were the persuasion approaches of the two, and what evidence can you provide to support your conclusions?

■   What were Colin's and John's objectives and how successful were they in achieving them?

■   What role did body language play, and how did it affect the way the meeting developed?

■   Imagine you were in Colin's shoes and faced with the same problem. What would you do differently and why?

Rather than moving straight into structured answers, which might reduce your inclination to come up with some thoughts yourself(!),

I want initially to consider some of the broader management aspects.

There was a lack of clarity in the relationship between Colin, the client and John. Accountability and responsibility were unclear, which meant that there had been no effective delegation of the task from Colin to John. While John had many failings, there was no suggestion that he couldn't do the job. Colin seemed to dip in and out of the task. So it was a kind of hands-on (without doing the work) then hands-off when distracted by his other responsibilities and then hands-on again. The trigger for Colin's occasional involvement was the client, happy not to pay for work already done, but keen to gain the information needed. The client communicated by writing directly to John, and then phoning Colin.

As good managers, we appreciate that work is delegated effectively when there has been a transference of responsibility and authority, but retention of accountability. This means a process of coaching and support until the subordinate has gained confidence and competence – from hands-on to hands-off, from control through support to monitoring that agreed targets are met.

Colin was stuck in this process, a situation fully exploited by John.

Another general point, to which we will return in the final chapter, concerns objectives. These need to be precise as to nature and timing. Colin managed a degree of precision on time (there was confusion between three and four weeks), but failed on the content side. Phrases like 'the majority of the information' are far too vague and serve neither the client nor the subordinate.

Turning now to the particular persuasion situation, it is interesting to consider the outcome in game theory terms. Depending on perspective and time, we could actually envisage a number of different outcomes. We could go for win/win. Colin's immediate objective was to persuade his subordinate (yes – Colin was the boss!) to complete the outstanding work in an agreed time.

From his point of view, if we gloss over the vague nature of the objectives agreed with John at the end of the discussion, he was successful, as he stated afterwards. Other related objectives were to get the bill paid as soon as possible and develop more business with the client. The relationship with the client, typical of many companies, was the senior man as the up-front friendly interface with the client, and the business developer, and the juniors as the work processors. Problems occurred when the work process was inadequate. This sort of rigid status division is not optimal, and more of a team approach, where the juniors are more involved with the client and gain a greater insight into client strategy and needs, is better all round.

John's objective was to do as little as possible as infrequently as possible. He was pleased, as the chances were he would do little late and get away with it. In fact, he felt confident he would be able to work on Colin's increasing level of anxiety and transfer some of the actual task upwards.

At the other end of the spectrum, we could argue that the outcome was in fact lose/lose. Colin would not get the work done when he expected – he had been given a verbal commitment only by John (one of many previously), which would not be followed up by effective action. Colin was an example (not that rare) of a non-assertive boss – in his case a preference in Empathy (of the non-assertive type) moderate Logic (rational in nature) with low Incentives and moderate Group. The profile is set out in Figure 46. There is a weak external focus. Colin was a man who avoided confrontation, found control difficult, and while genuinely supportive, fell over rather than standing up straight. There was little use of Incentives to provide structure and control to balance the support.

John, on the other hand, was a manipulator when in the followership role – moderate Empathy (a well-developed ability to read people), low Group, and preferences in Logic and Incentives. In the boss role, John's use of Incentives would have been much greater. He had a moderate internal focus. John's profile is shown in Figure 47.

We could think of John as losing, because he thinks he has won. If his desire for an easy life was too strong, he could be lulled into a false sense of security, based on extrapolation of the past. He could fail to read the warning signs – a boss becoming a little bit more assertive, due to the pressure from the client. A boss who, finding John lacking once again, could explode in frustration, with the added dimension of John's incompetence not only exacerbating the problem with the client, but bringing his own boss into play. The worm does turn or individuals who are non-assertive for too long often turn aggressive, when their backs are against the wall. At the end of the day, Colin was the boss, and had that positional power to use.

Turning to body language, we see how powerful it is both in influencing outcomes and in providing signals for the observant to read and use.

One small point, which was critical, was the positioning of the chairs. They were too close. When John's and Colin's feet were on the ground, they were invading each other's personal space. They

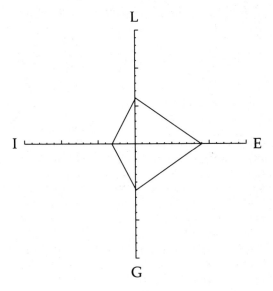

Figure 46 Colin's profile

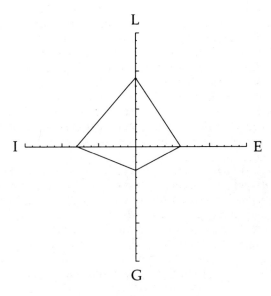

Figure 47 John's profile

did not move their chairs away from each other, which could have been one response. Instead, they leaned away from each other. This was a permanent feature of Colin's posture. John was slightly more positive, and while leaning away with his back used his body from the shoulder up to impose his body language on Colin.

Generally, John's good listening posture supported by nods and murmurs, his open gestures, forward movement to make his points, occasional pauses and direct eye contact all helped him thwart Colin's attempts to get him to admit to shortcomings, and to minimise the burden of work that passed his way.

On the other hand, on a couple of occasions, John's involuntary clusters indicated clearly that he was uncomfortable and prevaricating. If Colin had noticed these, he could have explored more deeply and might have gained the admission of historic incompetence and the commitment to improvement he desired.

Colin was uncomfortable throughout, retaining a defensive and protective posture, and while using direct eye contact and the occasional muted gesture when asking questions, always gave in when a potential crunch point arose.

Another problem for Colin was the unfortunate use of 'we', when it should have been 'I' or 'You'. It was occasionally an attempt at empathy, occasionally had a group aspect ie we should serve the client, but most of the time he meant 'You John should do this' or 'I want this'.

We must be so careful with our language, and say what we mean. Additionally, because of his non-assertive approach, Colin hedged and qualified, using a range of expressions such as 'obviously, maybe review, I think we need, probably, a little bit more urgency, possibly close on, fairly well planned, some commitment, give an indication'.

Another factor which hampered Colin was that nearly all his questions were closed, allowing John to provide yes or no answers with little amplification. Colin failed to follow up with any open questions, necessary to establish the truth.

It is surprising how difficult we find it to obtain the proper balance between open and closed questions. When we do an analysis of question types used in roleplays, there is invariably a bias in the question mix towards closed questions, with the occasional multiple, complicated, leading or loaded question. The few persuaders who are effective have a much higher proportion of open questions, and have developed the use of the pause to allow the persuadee to amplify their thinking and feelings or to commit to what they were avoiding!

Finally, if we stepped into Colin's shoes, how would we perform differently?

Colin admitted that he hadn't done much preparation, and was, naturally, nervous at being videoed as well as facing the situation he had encountered so often before, and so unsatisfactorily. He had briefed the other manager that John was quite able on the work front, but very lazy and always very polite, agreeable and positive in interviews. He would promise the earth at the drop of the hat, and deliver very little. John was a nice bloke, and they had developed a comfortable personal relationship.

So horses for courses. This is not the time to have a cosy comfortable chat. This is the time for a little distance. Let the desk re-appear, perhaps with John and Colin sitting side by side but not too close. This will give John an immediate message – food for thought. Colin should be professional and focused, with three objectives. First, John will have admitted that he has not performed as well as he should have done. Second he will answer the letter within a specified early time. Third, he will have provided the client with all the information within three weeks, copies of both letters to Colin.

Colin will need to structure the interview so that the main positive objectives are clearly defined and agreed. The facts should be established with closed questions. The emphasis should be on rational logic throughout. Deliberate use of direct questions and pauses to force a response will be required. Colin needs John to agree to the facts and the implications and, at the end, to know and accept what he is doing by what time, and what role he, Colin, will play.

Lets us have a stab at a replay. We will assume that Colin's body language is more positive and forceful, now he has the protection of the desk and a clear idea of what he wants to achieve and how. His tone should be friendly and firm. In the previous interview, John displayed a wide range of tone and modulation, whereas Colin was too flat and measured.

Colin: Good morning, John. Thank you for coming to see me. Do take a seat.

John: Good morning.

Colin: I have asked to see you so that together we agree an action plan to provide the information our major client, Marples, needs. Is that OK with you?

John: Of course, Colin. I'm happy to oblige. I don't see any problem with that. Just leave it to me.

Colin: What is the current position, John?

John: I've got everything in hand, Colin. The trouble is that they are such a pernickety client. They want all sorts of additional information like reports and accounts, which delays matters. (Colin pauses without speaking.) Their letter is at the top of my in-tray, and I'll get on to it straight away.

Colin: Let me see the letter. (John reluctantly hands it over. Colin takes time out to read the entire contents.) I see this letter is three weeks old. Can I see a copy of your reply?

John: Well, em, Colin, I have not replied yet, but I'll attend to it straight away. Top priority, Colin, I assure you.

Colin: This is a major client. They will not pay the invoices you have sent them over the last six months until they receive all the information requested in their letter. The outstanding information represents only a small part of a large fee, which we need for our cash-flow. I am getting pressure from them for action. Your lack of action is harming the relationship, and inhibits the development of new business. Do you agree that this is not a satisfactory position, John?

John: Well put like that, you have a point, Colin. (Colin pauses.) Perhaps I could have been a little more diligent, though I must say that they are a most pernickety client, unlike all my others.

Colin: (interrupting) But you do not have any other major clients. We re-allocated work within the section to leave you free to concentrate on Marples over a month ago.

John: (shuffling uncomfortably and looking away) Well, yes, Colin, you have good point. I'm sorry about that. I'll get on to it straight away, you can rest assured.

Colin: Fine, John. Apology accepted. Let us focus on future action. We need the information provided within three weeks, so that any queries can be ironed out, and our bill paid well before the end of their accounting year in three months. Will you be able to manage that?

John:	Yes, no problem, Colin.
Colin:	You will also need to write back to the client, acknowledging their letter and advising them exactly when they will receive all the information. Will you do that this afternoon, and send me a copy?
John:	Yes, of course, Colin.
Colin:	I would also like a copy of the final letter sent out in three weeks. Incidentally, that should include a request to settle the entire account. Is that OK with you, John?
John:	But of course, Colin. No problem at all.
Colin:	Another thing, John. As you rightly say, there is a lot of information to be researched and collected. My door is always open if I can be of help. I'll keep a copy of the letter so that I know the detail. Shall we put a date in our diaries for a week's time to review progress together, iron out any problems and ensure the three-week deadline is met, perhaps with a few days to spare, eh, John!
John:	Thanks, Colin, that would be helpful. I'll start the ball rolling now.
Colin:	Not so fast, John. Let's put the date of our next meeting in our diaries now and let's recap so that you and I are both sure as to who is doing what and when.

A different approach, the use of learned techniques and a different, better outcome for both parties. Colin is now using an approach to delegation that is appropriate for the situation and competence of this particular follower. Colin does not need to do the work, but does need to keep a tight control of the work flows. Equally, he provides the support that John needs. In leadership terms, Colin uses control with support.

John recognises that the game is up, but has not had his face rubbed in the dirt of historic incompetence, and has the ability, time and support from his leader to meet the targets set for him. He is beginning a development path that will make him more competent and effective. They are both moving towards a genuine win/win.

However, it is only a first significant step. If we were to stand back, we would notice that Colin had not developed nor used team leadership skills. Often the immediate need with managers is to develop either effective control to bolster the support or effective support to bolster the control. The reality of visionary team leadership is still far distant, though the need and the desire, as we saw in Chapter 4, is growing at both individual and organisational level, due to the seeds being sown by the whirlwind of change.

Additionally, it is unsatisfactory that Colin remains in the long term with such a degree of control over John, necessary in the short term. John will require coaching by Colin, perhaps bolstered by the appropriate training programme, so that John can discipline himself with deadlines and manage projects effectively with minimal support.

It is a powerful and positive reality that there are significant improvements in persuasion effectiveness through the passage of but a few hours and a little practice. Whether managers develop or revert when they have returned to the office depends largely on whether they create and apply their own action plan, the subject of the last chapter.

11

◆ Planning to Improve ◆

INTRODUCTION

In this final chapter, I provide some guidance to those who want to improve their competence as persuaders. I look at the whole improvement process, set out in four connected charts. While I will concentrate on persuasion, the approach holds for any area of improvement where how we behave affects how we perform.

CHANGE

The base point for improvement is self-knowledge. The more, and the more accurately, we know about our existing strengths and weaknesses in the given area, the better our ability to improve.

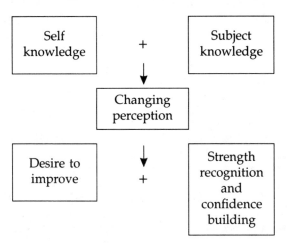

Figure 48 Change

Knowledge about self needs to be put into the context of knowledge about the subject area, so that we can determine what is possible in terms of future competence, as well as how our current performance measures up.

So the first two steps are gaining knowledge of self and the subject. This was the focus of the first four chapters of the book.

Most of us most of the time do not think explicitly about our competences. By gaining knowledge explicitly, we change our perception. We change our view of both our competence and our capability. Like Nazarrudin, we realise that there is something known as 'gold', and mere silver will no longer do. However, we should not lash ourselves emotionally with a perception of inadequacy nor sense of failure. We must recognise those strengths, which are always there.

It is worth stressing the reality of strength. Many underestimate themselves, either because of a non-assertive bias or because they set themselves absolute measures, and not measures based on relative performance. Invariably the vast majority of managers on effective programmes will recognise in themselves a degree and a depth of competence in a specific area that they had not appreciated before, but is visibly demonstrated by the performance of their peers.

Improvement comes from the recognition and development of strengths, which provides the confidence to tackle 'weaknesses'. In fact, often a weakness is just a strength used to excess.

An individual who has a well-developed, powerful, rational, logical approach to persuasion has a great strength. However, if that individual relies on rational logic with all people in all situations, that strength becomes a handicap. The underlying strength is always there. If the individual were to recognise this reality, the message should be: 'I need to develop capability in other approaches to persuasion to improve my overall competence, but I must appreciate the competence I have developed in logic, which I should develop, and not consider a weakness nor drawback to improvement'.

Incidentally, when it comes to an area where we are working predominantly on our own, like persuasion, we will need consciously to make comparisons with colleagues and friends. We will soon discover just how good we are at specific aspects of persuasion, whether logical thinking, the ability to use incentives to generate structure and discipline, well-developed individual or group creativity skills, good listening and questioning and so on.

This is very necessary, as psychology is at the heart of improvement – belief in self, self-confidence on the back of self-knowledge and strength recognition, coupled with the desire to improve and the belief in personal capability to achieve the improvements desired. You can drag a horse to water but you cannot make it drink. Change comes from within. Structure and methodology is essential to effective change, but if the psychological commitment and confidence is absent for whatever reason, then you have lots of water but no horse!

FOCUS

Desire needs to be supported by direction if change is going to be

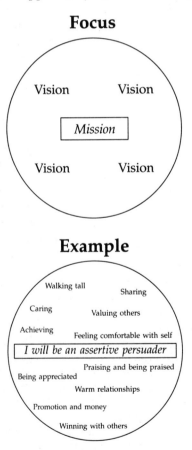

Figure 49 Focus and example

positive rather than random. This brings us to the next phase – developing a feel for where we want to be, now we know where we are and what can be achieved.

We need to set ourselves a mission, supported by a vision. Through this process, we can provide ourselves with focus and motivation. The visionary part is vital, as we will not improve with mere structure and system. We must generate drive and commitment to overcome the inertia from the past, and a sense of purpose and direction so that the momentum we achieve waxes rather than wanes.

As our example, we will say that our mission is to be an assertive persuader. We can generate a vision of what that means for us by concentrating on all the good things that will come our way when we succeed – picturing ourselves in situations and circumstances, where we enjoy the rewards, which feel and taste so good. Mental images are mighty motivators.

ACTION PLANNING

It is, however, insufficient to look up and say we must be there, when there is some distance away and we have no map nor compass. So we must fill in that gap, break down the journey into easy stages, so we know where we are going tomorrow and the next day and the next day.

As set out in Figure 50, the first step is to identify key results areas, which might be questioning, listening, creativity, assertiveness, and planning for meetings. The essence of good time management is to identify those few vital areas of activity, which mean that, if we do them well, we have done our job well. We then focus our actions in those key areas, and not in the host of activities that can crowd out our days, and yet generate so little progress. This general truth holds for a given development area like persuasion.

In addition to identifying those key action areas that are relevant for you (not ignoring that some will be successes already, which need to be acknowledged and further strengthened), I suggest in the chart that you should set goals. It is not really necessary, as they can be taken for granted though often appearing in job descriptions as a substitute for objectives! A goal is a verbal aspiration, and the words we tend to use are 'to enhance', 'to develop', 'to improve'. Apple-pie and motherhood! It is objectives or targets or milestones that make the difference. These, as mentioned in Chapter 9, provide the short- and medium-term focus to action, as

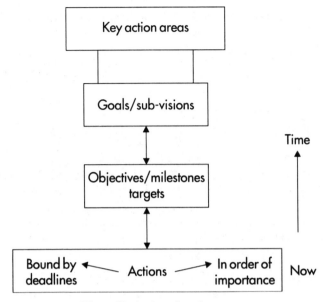

Figure 50 Action planning

they measure progress, are bound by time, and provide stretch, context and direction. While goals tend to be obvious and add little value – after all, if we are going to spend time in the 'listening area', we are highly unlikely to be reducing our listening competence rather than improving it(!), visioning is more powerful. In other words, we can imagine what success feels like in a given action area to improve our motivation. We can create a sub-vision in a key action area that develops and reinforces the overall vision, supporting the mission.

Let me at this stage put a pragmatic hat on, and provide two specific examples, one in listening and one in questioning.

Listening

While it is easy to set objectives in such 'hard' areas like sales (we will increase our sales by 20 per cent in one year), it is much more difficult to do so in 'soft' areas like listening.

However, what we cannot measure, we cannot easily manage. How can we achieve our mission, if we cannot measure progressive success in the key action areas?

We have to be imaginative. Here is one possible series of

objectives, taking our time-horizon to achieve our listening goal as six months.

- After six months I will ask five people I know (whom I will select randomly at the time from a shortlist of twenty) whether they think I have become a better listener. They will all say yes and when asked to estimate the degree of change state that my improvement is at least 50 per cent, compared with six months previously.
- At the end of five months, I will be consciously and actively listening at the rate of ten times a day.
- At the end of three months, I will be consciously and actively listening at the rate of five times a day.

Next we determine the actions and the order needed to achieve these objectives. These will vary from individual to individual, but one set could be, putting in order but not adding the specific deadlines required in practice:

- Carry out research and obtain information eg purchase of good book on body language, exercises on listening, access to video equipment.
- Read key information and note key points.
- Draw up action plan.
- Carry out exercises with trusted friend (using video equipment if possible). A series of exercises that would be useful are:
  — Ask her to speak to you for four minutes on a topic of interest, listen as well as you can (no words allowed) and then summarise what she said. Obtain feedback both as to accuracy of summary and how effective she felt your listening was. Critically, discover what were the good aspects and the not so good.
  — Reverse the roles and repeat the procedure.
  — Revert to the original format, but this time ask your friend to talk about something close to her heart, and, without telling her, deliberately and slowly (without exaggeration) move into ineffective listening – glancing away, closing body posture and so on. This will have a marked impact on your friend, and is a powerful learning device, when the emotions as well as the body language (of both parties) are reviewed.

    A video recording is not vital, but does help underline the messages in visual form, which adds greater impact. It also allows review and reinforcement at a later date.

- Determine your approach to conscious active listening.

■ Carry out conscious listening on two occasions in a day, and record your feelings and how you perceive the other party reacted.

■ Continue building up to the required number a day by the required time.

There are one or two other things to think about, before we have finished with the listening aspect, but these are covered in the final section Connection and Integration. First, we look at questioning in a similar way.

Questioning

The six-month objective could be similar to your listening objective, which means that when you ask about your listening skills, you should ask about your questioning skills at the same time. This demonstrates the importance of having an integrated approach. We should not focus on each action area in isolation. Before carrying out a single action in any area, we need to work out where the connections are between areas and what is the optimal degree and nature of integration.

You may recall that I referred in Chapter 5 to the art of listening and the science of questioning. People know instinctively whether someone is a good or bad listener. This is because listening is fundamentally an emotionally based activity, which is why body language and not words(!) is the key to both recognition and development. Questioning is less emotional and more rational. Rational activities need factual knowledge. If you opt for a six-month questioning objective similar to the six-month listening objective, you may need to educate your colleagues or friends into what constitutes good questioning before they can assess you. (You could always buy them copies of this book!)

If this seems too complicated, an alternative is to set yourself progressively more demanding targets over time, whereby you increase your use of open questions, and decrease use of closed, multiple, complicated, 'or' questions, staccato, leading, and loaded questions.

To meet such objectives, the immediate need will be to develop recognition of each type of question. This is not too difficult. This book should be sufficient to enable you to know what each is. Complete comfort will come from consciously observing others in conversation (not initially yourself) and noting the pattern of questioning and the frequency each type is used. This may sound a bit contrived, but you will find it is not. You will also find just how frequently others use the wrong question mix and type, and how that limits their persuasion competence.

Once the knowledge base is established with appropriate actions, you can then turn to yourself. It is difficult, though not impossible, to hold conversations when you are busy noting down which question type you and the other person are using. Getting permission to take notes is a necessary first step.

Alternatives, which need not be exclusive, are to use the mirror in hypothetical persuasion situations with a hypothetical per-suadee (which can actually be a lot of fun and is also an excellent approach in the latter stages of development, when you are preparing for the real vital persuasion meeting) or the services of a good friend and video equipment if possible. The latter is also a lot of fun. Learning shared is more powerful and the friend gains as much as you.

Finally, in this area, observing others acts as an effective way of improving yourself, as well as confirming question types initially, and can be deployed throughout.

CONNECTION AND INTEGRATION

Listening and questioning areas are unlikely to be the only key results areas we have identified. We will need to ensure that we do not overstretch ourselves. Pace is all important. Rome was not built

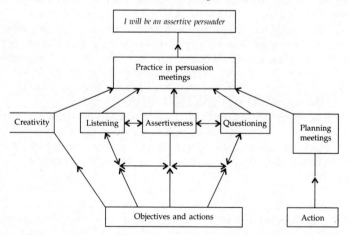

Figure 51 Connection and integration

in a day, nor for that matter in seven days. There is a real danger that we will start off like cheetahs and only cheat ourselves of success. One step at a time is essential.

There are lasting benefits from being assertive persuaders or VTLs. They will only be obtained if we go slowly and carefully and do not overload ourselves. This is especially true if we have busy professional lives. The reality is that personal improvement is, initially, an extra time cost. I say initially, as fairly soon improved competence in persuasion saves time. Getting it right first time, the key to effectiveness in any area, always saves time, and eventually saves money.

So we need to prioritise our key action areas. Listening and questioning should come first. They should be connected at some stage, when we are practising, as they complement each other. This is why I have linked questioning and listening part way along their separate journeys. If we are tackling assertiveness, then we should not start until we have progressed in our questioning and listening skills, which will form a significant part of improving assertiveness. Equally, when we are developing assertiveness, then we should incorporate practice in questioning and listening in the assertiveness actions, rather than in isolation. This is why I have linked both questioning and listening to assertiveness.

Integration develops as we develop. Creative thinking can be separate for most of the journey with practice in isolation or interpersonal interaction as with the other development areas, but all come together when we start improving our competence in real persuasion meetings. Prior to this final stage, we will need to consider planning. Here I have just indicated the action of planning, as we do not need to set objectives in planning. When planning, we set objectives for the meeting.

CONCLUSION

Well, that's it. This particular journey has reached its natural conclusion. It is one that I have enjoyed for many reasons that are evidenced by my own profile, which I produced from the ILEG Inventory. I also persuaded my wife to fill in the 'other' ILEG Inventory, so that I could contrast and compare. The result was a change in perception and desire to improve.

You have briefly considered that profile in the first chapter – John. John was a man who could confuse vision and ego, who could find himself half-way down the hill when his followers were still climbing it, who could demotivate immature followers, and who needed to become more empathetic. He had important strengths in rational logic, creativity, team focus and visioning.

So I must away to formulate and implement my own action plan!

◆ Recommended Reading ◆

Adair, J (1988) *Effective Leadership*, (rev ed) Pan, London

Blanchard, K, PhD and Johnson, S, MD (1983) *The One Minute Manager*, Fontana/Collins, London

Back, K and K (1982) *Assertiveness at Work*, McGraw-Hill, Maidenhead

Biddle, D and Evenden, R (1988) *Human Aspects of Management* (2nd ed), Institute of Personnel Management, London

Brown, JAC (1963) *Techniques of Persuasion: From Propaganda to Brainwashing*, Penguin, London

Buzan, T (1989) *Use Your Head* (rev ed), BBC, London

De Bono, E (1982) *Lateral Thinking for Management*, Penguin, London

De Bono, E (1987) *Six Thinking Hats*, Pelican, London

Drucker, P F (1967) *The Effective Executive*, Heinemann Professional Publishing, London

Fisher, R and Ury, W (1986) *Getting to Yes: Negotiating Agreement Without Giving In*, Hutchinson Business, London

Harris, T A (1973) *I'm OK – You're OK*, Pan, London

Harvey-Jones, J (1988) *Making it Happen: Reflections on Leadership*, Fontana/Collins, London

Hermann, N (1988) *The Creative Brain*, Brain Books, Lace Lure, North Carolina US

Honey, P (1980) *Solving People Problems*, McGraw-Hill, Maidenhead

Hunt, J (1981) *Managing People at Work: A Manager's Guide to Behaviour in Organisations*, Pan, London

Mackay, I (1984) *A Guide to Listening*, Bacie, London

Parikh, J (1991) *Managing Your Self: Management by Detached Involvement*, Basil Blackwell, Oxford

Pease, A (1981) *Body Language: How to Read Others' Thoughts by Their Gestures*, Sheldon Press, London

Scott, B (1987) *The Skills of Communicating*, Gower, Aldershot

Index

rule for effective group creativity, 133

self-deceiver persuasion profile, 52
staccato style of questioning, 112–13
staff attitude survey, 137, 146
sub-antarctic survival situation, 95–6
Sundridge Park Management Centre, 81, 92, 159
support leadership orientation, 20, 70, 89

team exercises
  counterplay, 152

sub-antarctic survival situation, 95–6
technical role, 83
Thatcher, Margaret, 38
Touche Ross survey, 44

vision, 116, 175, 176
vision leadership orientation, 20, 70, 90
visionary persuasion profile, 51
visionary team leader (VTL), 73, 74, 75, 80, 88, 90, 91, 115–16, 139

Zigarni, Drea on situational leadership, 84